Composition: models and exercises

C

Composition:
models and exercises

DIANE A. WILBUR
PHILIP McFARLAND

**SECOND
EDITION**

DESMOND J. NUNAN
Consulting Editor

JOHN E. WARRINER
General Editor

HARCOURT BRACE JOVANOVICH, INC.

New York   Chicago   San Francisco   Atlanta   Dallas

THE AUTHORS

DIANE A. WILBUR has been a teacher of English in grades 7 through 12. She has also been an instructor in the English Department at Wayne State University.

PHILIP McFARLAND has taught English for a number of years at Concord Academy, Concord, Massachusetts. Earlier he served as an editor in educational publishing. He is the author of the novel *A House Full of Women.*

CONSULTING EDITOR

DESMOND J. NUNAN is Assistant to the Superintendent in the Allentown (Pa.) School District. Previously he was Director of Curriculum in the West Chester Public Schools for three years and taught English for twelve years in both public and private schools. He majored in English at Columbia College and received his doctorate from the University of Pennsylvania.

GENERAL EDITOR

JOHN E. WARRINER has taught English for thirty-two years in junior and senior high schools and in college. He is the chief author of the *English Grammar and Composition* series and a coauthor of the *English Workshop* series.

ACKNOWLEDGMENTS: *For permission to reprint copyrighted material, grateful acknowledgment is made to the following publishers, authors, and agents:*

AMERICAN HERITAGE PUBLISHING CO., INC.: "The Most Mysterious Manuscript," by Alfred Werner, © copyright 1963 by American Heritage Publishing Co., Inc. in *Horizon* Magazine of January 1963.
APPLETON-CENTURY-CROFTS, EDUCATIONAL DIVISION, MEREDITH CORPORATION: "Charles Dickens: The Boy of the London Streets" by Rupert Sargent Holland from *St. Nicholas Magazine,* 1909.
ATHENEUM PUBLISHERS: From *The Empty Space* by Peter Brook, published by Atheneum, copyright © 1968 by Peter Brook.
ESTATE OF JOHN MASON BROWN and THE SATURDAY REVIEW: "I Hate the Comics" by John Mason Brown in *Saturday Review of Literature,* March 20, 1948, copyright 1948 The Saturday Review Associates, Inc.
CHANNEL PRESS, AFFILIATE OF MEREDITH PRESS: "Washington Irving: A National Asset" by Claude G. Bowers in *The Unforgettable Americans,* edited by John A. Garraty, copyright © 1960 by Broadcast Music, Inc.
THOMAS Y. CROWELL COMPANY, NEW YORK: "Canoes" in *Beginning with Boats*

Contents

SECTION TWO: DESCRIPTION

SECTION THREE: NARRATION

SECTION FOUR: EXPOSITION

SECTION SEVEN: WRITING ABOUT LITERATURE

The Paragraph

LESSON **1**

Unity in Paragraphs

Although paragraphs vary in kind and length, every effective paragraph is unified. A unified paragraph is one in which all the sentences contained within it work toward a common goal. This lesson lets you examine three kinds of paragraphs to see how each achieves unity.

UNITY IN A DESCRIPTIVE PARAGRAPH   The first model is a description of a building on a university campus. In reading it, notice that the writer concentrates on details that together create a single, unified impression.

1   **Evan S. Connell, Jr. in "The Anatomy Lesson"**

North Fayer Hall stood on the final and lowest hill of the university, a little askew from the other buildings as if it were ashamed of its shabbiness and had turned partly away. Its window sills were pocked by cigarette burns, and the doors of its green tin lockers had been pried open for so many years that few of them would lock any more; the creaking floors were streaked and spattered with drops of paint, dust lay upon the skylights, and because the ventilating system could not carry off so many fumes it seemed forever drenched in turpentine. Mercifully the little building was hidden each afternoon by the shadows of its huge, ivy-jacketed companions.

The Writer's Craft

1. The description begins by noting that North Fayer Hall seemed "ashamed of its shabbiness." What follows are details that convey the shabbiness of the building: window sills pocked by cigarette burns, lockers that no longer lock. What other details in the paragraph help convey an impression of the building's shabbiness?

2. Do all the sentences contribute to the impression of shabbiness? Does that impression give the paragraph unity?

3. Suppose this sentence had appeared in the paragraph: "The funds to erect North Fayer Hall had been given to the school by a local banker named Broderick R. Fayer." Does the statement relate to the shabbiness of the building? How would the addition of the sentence affect the unity of the paragraph?

Now You Try It

Choose one of the following:

1. Select a subject from those listed below, or a subject of your own, to describe in a paragraph of 100 to 200 words. Before you begin the paragraph, list the details you plan to use. Write your paragraph only after you have examined each detail to make sure it contributes to the picture or the impression you want to create.

    a. The gymnasium the morning after a dance
    b. The locker room ten minutes before a game
    c. My first-grade teacher
    d. The house I would like to live in
    e. A store in our neighborhood

2. Write a unified descriptive paragraph using one of the following as the first sentence. If you prefer, you may make up your own opening sentence.

    a. _____ has the most interesting face I know.
    b. Everything in the room looked unused and unusable.
    c. _____ is a disturbing place to visit.
    d. "Hectic" is the only word for our corridors between classes.
    e. My bedroom reflects my interests.

UNITY IN A NARRATIVE PARAGRAPH   A narrative tells a story or brings an experience to life. The following is an example of a unified narrative paragraph.

2   Ernest Hemingway in "On the Blue Water"

An old man fishing alone in a skiff * out of Cabanas °
hooked a great marlin that, on the heavy sashcord
line, pulled the skiff far out to sea. Two days later the
old man was picked up by fishermen sixty miles to the
eastward, the head and forward part of the marlin
lashed alongside. What was left of the fish, less than
half, weighed eight hundred pounds. The old man had
stayed with him a day, a night, a day, and another
night while the fish swam deep and pulled the boat.
When he had come up, the old man had pulled the
boat up on him and harpooned him. Lashed alongside,
the sharks had hit him and the old man had fought
them out alone in the Gulf Stream in a skiff, clubbing
them, stabbing at them, lunging at them with an oar
until he was exhausted and the sharks had eaten all
that they could hold. He was crying in the boat when
the fishermen picked him up, half crazy from his loss,
and the sharks were still circling the boat.

* **skiff:** a light, open rowboat.
° **Cabanas:** a village in Cuba.

The Writer's Craft

1. The paragraph tells what happened when an old man
caught a giant marlin. Is every sentence in it related to that single
event?

2. Could either of the following sentences be added without
destroying the unity of the paragraph? Explain your answer.

> Although they live in all parts of the ocean, sharks are
> most numerous in warm waters.

> The old man knew more about fishing than anyone else in
> Cabanas.

Choose one of the following:

1. Develop one of the incidents listed below in a unified narrative paragraph.

    a. A funny thing that happened at school
    b. Winning an election
    c. The most exciting play of a football game
    d. Making a new friend
    e. Taking advantage of an unexpected opportunity

2. Begin a brief narrative paragraph with one of the statements below. Be sure all your other sentences are related to the single event or mood referred to at the start.

    a. I vividly remember my first (roller coaster ride, gym class, dance, visit to the circus, overnight camping trip).
    b. I sat in the car wondering if we would ever get there.
    c. I had never been so frightened in my life.
    d. Once I decided that I too could bake a cake.
    e. Until I began my speech, I had not felt at all nervous.

UNITY IN AN EXPOSITORY PARAGRAPH The following paragraph is expository; that is, its primary purpose is to explain something. Like all effective expository paragraphs, it is built around a unifying idea. As you read, see whether every sentence helps develop that idea.

3 James Ramsey Ullman in "Why Men Climb Toward the Skies"

Mountaineering, to be sure, means many different and often opposing things to its different practitioners. For an adventurous specialized few, it means ambitious expeditions and first ascents — Alaska, the Andes, the Himalayas. For another comparatively small group, it means an interest in complex climbing problems and the development and refinement of techniques. And for the rest of us — most of us — it means simply to visit mountains when and where we can and to climb them according to our opportunities and abilities whether it be among Alps or Adirondacks, Catskills or Karakorams.

The Writer's Craft

1. The central idea in Ullman's paragraph is that mountaineering means different things to the various people who practice it. Do all the sentences in the paragraph help support that idea, or are some unrelated details included? Has the author written a unified paragraph? Explain your answer.

2. Suppose the paragraph had been written this way:

> Mountaineering, to be sure, means many different and often opposing things to its different practitioners. *Sports car racing and swimming are similar in that they also mean different things to different people.* For an adventurous specialized few, it means ambitious expeditions and first ascents — Alaska, the Andes, the Himalayas. *The Himalayas are beautiful to look at but treacherous to climb.* For another comparatively small group, it means an interest in complex climbing problems and the development and refinement of techniques. And for the rest of us — most of us — it means simply to visit mountains when and where we can and to climb them according to our opportunities and abilities whether it be among Alps or Adirondacks, Catskills or Karakorams.

How do the italicized sentences affect the unity of the paragraph? Explain your answer.

Now You Try It

The following sentences might serve as statements of ideas that could unify expository paragraphs. Choose one sentence, then add to it several more of your own in order to develop a brief unified paragraph. Be sure that every sentence you add supports the unifying idea.

a. School means different things to different people.
b. Experience is a good teacher.
c. Water is essential to life.
d. It is hard to value highly anything that comes too easily.
e. Astronauts are exceptionally courageous men.

LESSON

The Topic Sentence

Expository paragraphs — those that inform or explain — often use a device called the topic sentence, which expresses the unifying or main idea of the paragraph. To appreciate the importance of the topic sentence, read the following paragraph; the topic sentence has been removed from it.

> Noise tapped away at the bullfrog until his ears became bigger than his eyes. Now he hears so well that at the slightest sound of danger he quickly plops to safety under a sunken leaf. The rabbit has long ears to hear the quiet "whoosh" of the owl's wings. The grasshopper's ears are on the base of his abdomen, the lowest point of his body, where he can detect the tread of a crow's foot or the stealthy approach of a shrew.

In reading the sentences above you probably sense that they are related. But can you tell exactly how? Do you know what the unifying idea of the paragraph is?

Now read the same paragraph with the topic sentence restored.

4 **Jean George**
in "That Astounding Creator — Nature"

> Sound has shaped the bodies of many beasts. Noise tapped away at the bullfrog until his ears became bigger than his eyes. Now he hears so well that at the

slightest sound of danger he quickly plops to safety under a sunken leaf. The rabbit has long ears to hear the quiet "whoosh" of the owl's wings. The grasshopper's ears are on the base of his abdomen, the lowest point of his body, where he can detect the tread of a crow's foot or the stealthy approach of a shrew.

With the topic sentence (*Sound has shaped the bodies of many beasts*) in place, the paragraph is focused clearly. Now you understand the underlying idea behind the mention of the bullfrog's, the rabbit's, and the grasshopper's ears, whereas without the topic sentence the paragraph seems to be merely a series of statements about the ears of different animals.

THE TOPIC SENTENCE AT THE BEGINNING OF A PARAGRAPH   In Model 4 the topic sentence is the first in the paragraph. This is the position it frequently assumes, although sometimes it is placed in the middle or at the end of a paragraph — or it may even be left out entirely if the unifying idea is perfectly clear despite the omission. Placed at the beginning, the topic sentence establishes the unifying idea at once and guides the development of what follows. Notice the value of the initial topic sentence in the paragraph below.

5   Robert P. Tristram Coffin in *Kennebec*

You can't be sure of Maine weather. The farmers reckon it lucky if they can get their beans in by Decoration Day. Even then, June may turn out frosty. Any full moon is almost sure to bring along a silver blanket that leaves the tomatoes looking like the last slice of bacon on a side-slab. There's one month, Maine folks say, when you can count on having no frost — July. I believed that till last Fourth of July. I had to set out my marigolds over again after that.

1. Compare the following versions of Coffin's paragraph with the original. In the first version the topic sentence appears in the middle of the paragraph, and in the second it appears at the end.

> The farmers in Maine reckon it lucky if they can get their beans in by Decoration Day. Even then, June may turn out frosty. Any full moon is almost sure to bring along a silver blanket that leaves the tomatoes looking like the last slice of bacon on a side-slab. *You can't be sure of Maine weather.* There's one month, Maine folks say, when you can count on having no frost — July. I believed that till last Fourth of July. I had to set out my marigolds over again after that.

> The farmers in Maine reckon it lucky if they can get their beans in by Decoration Day. Even then, June may turn out frosty. Any full moon is almost sure to bring along a silver blanket that leaves the tomatoes looking like the last slice of bacon on a side-slab. There's one month, Maine folks say, when you can count on having no frost — July. I believed that till last Fourth of July. I had to set out my marigolds over again after that. *You can't be sure of Maine weather.*

What is the effect of placing the topic sentence in the middle of the paragraph? at the end of the paragraph?

2. Why is the beginning a good position for the topic sentence in Coffin's paragraph?

Here is a paragraph that describes an aspect of life in Toluca, a provincial Mexican town, in 1919. Again, the topic sentence is at the beginning.

6 Langston Hughes in *The Big Sea*

The weekly movie show was a gala occasion for the whole town. Society and its pretty daughters attended and sat in the horseshoe of circular boxes, running from one side of the stage to the other around the ancient auditorium. The young blades and unmarried males of the better families sat in the orchestra proper, and between each reel of bad Hollywood movies, or arty German ones, practically all the males would rise and sweep the circle of boxes with their eyes until they found the girl each liked. Then they would stare at her until the house went dark again. The shows commenced at four o'clock and lasted an ungodly long time, because they had only one projector and had to show each picture reel by reel. When the sun went down, it got very cold in Toluca, and the old theater had no heat, but you gathered your coat about you and stuck it out until the last cowboy had killed the last redskin and smothered the heroine in a kiss. Then you came home through the badly lighted streets, where the meek Indian policemen, huddled in blankets to the eyebrows, slept leaning against adobe corners, a lantern on the ground at their feet.

The Writer's Craft

1. What idea does the topic sentence in this paragraph express? Do the remainder of the sentences in the paragraph help develop that idea? Is the paragraph unified?

2. Could the following sentence be added to the paragraph without destroying its unity? Explain.

> As for myself, I received an allowance of ten pesos a week, but there was nothing much to spend money for in such a quiet little town.

Now You Try It

1. A topic sentence should express an idea limited enough to be developed within a paragraph. The sentence "You can learn about human nature just by watching people" states so broad an idea that a single paragraph could hardly develop it adequately. However, you might change the sentence to read: "You can learn about human nature just by watching people in a bus station." The mention of a specific place limits the topic enough so that it could be developed comfortably within a paragraph.

Listed below are five broad topic sentences. Rewrite each one, narrowing the topic so that it can be adequately developed in a single paragraph. Each specimen can be narrowed by making it more specific. In the first sentence, for example, you would probably mention a specific area of behavior in which you think teenagers should have more freedom.

a. Teen-agers should be allowed more freedom.
b. Team sports demand greater skill than individual sports do.
c. Trips to historical places are interesting.
d. School is challenging.
e. People are capable of cruelty to each other.

2. Compose a paragraph of 100–200 words developing one of the revised topic sentences you wrote for exercise 1. Place the topic sentence first in the paragraph and be sure that each sentence you include after it is closely related to the topic.

THE TOPIC SENTENCE AT THE END OF A PARAGRAPH   Although the topic sentence is frequently placed first, there are times when an end position is more effective, as in the following paragraph.

7   Edwin Way Teale in "Beneficent Cannibalism"

It makes no sound; it is voiceless. It turns its pointed face this way and that; it is the only insect that can turn its head like a man. It merges with the foliage of its background; its body is camouflaged in greens and browns. It remains for long periods with forearms uplifted as though in supplication; it is thus that it awaits the approach of its victims. This creature of curious attributes is the praying mantis, known in various localities as the Soothsayer, the Nun, or the Devil's Rearhorse.

The Writer's Craft

1. Teale mentions four characteristics of a creature before telling you, in the concluding sentence, what that creature is. Does placing the topic sentence at the end make the paragraph

more interesting? Before answering, compare the original with the following version of the paragraph, in which the topic sentence has been slightly adapted to be placed at the beginning.

> Known in various localities as the Soothsayer, the Nun, or the Devil's Rearhorse, the praying mantis is a creature of curious attributes. It makes no sound; it is voiceless. It turns its pointed face this way and that; it is the only insect that can turn its head like a man. It merges with the foliage of its background; its body is camouflaged in greens and browns. It remains for long periods with forearms uplifted as though in supplication; it is thus that it awaits the approach of its victims.

Do you prefer the topic sentence at the beginning or at the end of the paragraph? Give reasons for your answer.

2. To change the location of the topic sentence in the rewritten version, Teale's original sentence had to be altered. In what ways? Why were the alterations necessary? (Hint: Put Teale's original sentence first and see what happens.)

Now You Try It

The topic sentence of Model 7 not only identified the praying mantis but also summarized details about the insect given in the preceding sentences. Below are several sentences, each of which could act as a summary statement for a series of details. Select one as a topic sentence and write a paragraph in which it appears at the end. You do not have to create a riddle, as Teale did in Model 7, but you may if you wish.

- a. Thus through volunteer work teen-agers can show they have a sense of responsibility.
- b. For all those reasons athletics are an important part of the school program.
- c. It proves that a sense of humor can help put problems in perspective.
- d. Again I was reminded that popular music does express some emotions very well.
- e. For the first time I understood that allowances are meant to teach the importance of planning ahead.
- f. So if you plan your viewing, you will discover that television is a worthwhile way to spend time.

THE CLINCHER SENTENCE In some paragraphs the main idea, expressed at the beginning in a topic sentence, is restated in different words at the end. The restatement has been called a clincher sentence, because its purpose is to summarize or clinch the main idea. Both of the paragraphs that follow illustrate the device.

8   Bergen Evans in "The Road to Vulgarity"

Our speech is probably more crammed with clichés today than ever before. The torrent of printed and recorded matter that is dumped on us every hour in the newspapers and from radio and television is bound to be repetitious and stereotyped. The brightest, gabbiest day in the world's history never produced one millionth, in fresh, original, and honest expression, of the bulk of what cascades over us every day. All of this stuff is of necessity prepared in furious haste. There is neither time nor energy for care or thought and the inevitable result is a huge heap of clichés.

9   Woodrow Wilson in *The New Freedom*

When I look back on the processes of history, when I survey the genesis of America, I see this written over every page: that the nations are renewed from the bottom, not from the top; that the genius which springs up from the ranks of unknown men is the genius which renews the youth and energy of the people. Everything I know about history, every bit of experience and observation that has contributed to my thought, has confirmed me in the conviction that the real wisdom of human life is compounded out of the experience of ordinary man. The utility, the vitality, the fruitage of life does not come from the top to the bottom. It comes, like the natural growth of a great tree, from the soil, up through the trunk into the branches to the foliage and the fruit. The great struggling unknown masses of the men who are at the base of everything are the dynamic force that is lifting the levels of society. A nation is as great, and only as great, as her rank and file.

The Writer's Craft

1. In the paragraphs by Evans and President Wilson the clincher sentences are not exact restatements of the topic sentences. How do the two types of sentence differ in each model? In your opinion, is the difference desirable?

2. On the basis of your analysis of models 8 and 9, what would you say were the advantages of using both a topic sentence and a clincher sentence in a paragraph? Should the device be used frequently? Justify your answer.

Now You Try It

From the list of topic sentences below, choose one to develop in a brief paragraph. If you prefer, you may write a topic sentence of your own. Begin the paragraph with the topic sentence, and end it with a summarizing clincher sentence.

- a. Travel is educational.
- b. You can learn a good deal about history from reading biographies.
- c. Ignorance is a breeding ground for fear.
- d. People who are sure of themselves are not afraid to make mistakes.
- e. The problems of living in cities are becoming more numerous and more urgent.

LESSON **3**

Paragraph Development

As you have seen, the topic sentence states the main idea of an expository paragraph. As for the other sentences in the paragraph, their function very often is to develop or support that central idea with specific details. What kinds of details should be included? Depending upon one's purpose in writing, the nature of a particular topic sentence, and the material at hand, the details used can be examples, incidents, or reasons. Or they can be all three, for though treated separately in this lesson for purposes of illustration, these different kinds of details are often effectively combined within a single paragraph. The question for you to consider in developing a paragraph is not so much what kind of detail to use but how to give adequate support to the main idea of your paragraph.

DEVELOPMENT WITH EXAMPLES Examples provide one effective way to develop a paragraph. In the following model, notice the many examples that illustrate the point made in the topic sentence.

10   Robert P. Tristram Coffin in "My Best Uncle"

Uncle Thomas took me with him on fishing trips and told me the things I ought to know. He taught me how to box the compass, tub a trawl, and name all the sails and lines on a full-rigged ship and what each one was for and how a score of men's lives could hang on one single knot. He schooled me in wind and weather, the two oldest and most important studies in the world. He told me how I could tell what winds were coming, by the feel of a spar, the looks of the clouds, or the way my head felt inside. He taught me how to look around a corner of one day into the next. The little streaks a cloud left were no bigger than the hairs on a paint brush, and yet they might mean life or death to you next day. He told me what secrets there were in the moon and how a man would die if he didn't watch her carefully to see what she was up to. He made my eyes stretch out to far headlands and blossoms of surf which meant trouble. He made my ears widen out and take in sounds of a low tune in the lines of the rigging. I learned about the sea and her woman tricks from Uncle Thomas. If she was on your side, you were safe. But you had to know her good side and stay on it.

The Writer's Craft

1. Which sentence in this paragraph is the topic sentence? What idea does that sentence express?

2. Find at least five examples that illustrate the idea stated in the topic sentence.

3. Would the paragraph be as effective if the author had given only the examples in the second and third sentences? Is there any limit, do you think, to the number of examples a writer should give within a single paragraph? If so, how would you determine that limit?

The following paragraph is about a tiny, mouselike animal called the shrew. The writer has developed the paragraph by giving examples of the ways in which the shrew is adapted to soil life.

11   Peter Farb in *Living Earth*

A shrew is perfectly adapted to soil life. Its snout is composed of bones that much resemble a plow. Its velvety fur never musses, even when the animal travels backward, a decided advantage for passing through the confines of narrow tunnels. The small black eyes, hidden deep inside the fur, are practically useless, and at most are only capable of distinguishing night from day. It is surprising that the eyes have survived at all, for the shrew has little need for them in its black tunnels where it relies on hearing and touch stimuli from its extraordinarily sensitive whiskers.

The Writer's Craft

1. What statement does the topic sentence make? How many examples are given to support that statement?

2. Are examples necessary in this paragraph? In other words, would you know how the shrew was adapted to soil life if the writer had not included the examples?

DEVELOPMENT WITH FACTS   Frequently the examples included to support the central idea of a paragraph are of a special kind — dates or proper names or statistical records or other such factual data. Although facts may be regarded as only another kind of example, nevertheless there is some value in noting that paragraphs may be developed in a strictly factual way, as in the following model, which considers American technology in the mid-nineteenth century.

12   Bernard De Voto in *The Year of Decision: 1846*

Look at the Patent Office. U. S. Pat. No. 4,464, April 18, 1846, to Royal C. House. A printing telegraph. Thus, two years after there was a public telegraph, long before there was a typewriter, there was a teletype. But what was significant in House's invention was the exquisite, exact, automatic production of successive operations in fixed sequence. Or U. S. Pat. No. 4,704, August 20, 1846, to Thomas J. Sloan. A simple thing: a wood screw which had a gimlet point and so turned itself into the wood instead of having to have a hole bored for it, the screw you used yesterday to put up a wall bracket. Or patent to Washburn Race of Seneca Falls, N. Y., for a self-acting register for stoves. Or patent to Erastus B. Bigelow, power loom for two- and three-ply ingrain carpets — next year he will patent looms for tapestries and Brussels carpets. Or a double handful of patents improving the textile machinery of Lowell, self-acting mules, new Jacquard Frames for figured fabrics, till one is dizzy making notes. Patent for hat-body machinery to H. A. Wells — and there are shifts and regroupings at Danbury. Patents to F. Langenheim of Philadelphia, W. A. Pratt of Alexandria, Virginia, and several others — improvements in the materials, processes, and mechanics for making reproductions by daguerreotype.

The Writer's Craft

1. Facts, of course, can be verified, or checked; that is what distinguishes a fact from an opinion. The facts in this paragraph are being used to illustrate the variety, inventiveness, and increasing sophistication of mid-nineteenth century American technology. Find at least four facts that the author includes to make his point about the vigor of American inventiveness in 1846. Do the facts convince you of that vigor?

2. Suppose the facts had been omitted, and the author had simply written:

> Look at the patent office records for 1846 and you will find there an amazing record of inventiveness, ranging over a wide variety of human activities and interests. Many extraordinary devices were invented that year, and others were refined and made more efficient and less cumbersome.

Is this paragraph as convincing as the writer's actual paragraph? Why, or why not?

The following paragraph is also developed with facts. See whether the support they give seems adequate.

13   Hudson Strode in *Denmark Is a Lovely Land*

The six children of Christian * and his German-born queen, Louise, made uncommonly good diplomatic marriages. One daughter, Alexandra, became Queen of England. Another, Dagmar, became the wife of Czar Alexander III and was known to Russia as the Czarina Maria Feodorovna. A third married the Duke of Cumberland. The eldest son, Frederik, who in time became king of Denmark, married Princess Louise, only daughter of Charles XV of Sweden. The second, George, who married the Grand Duchess Olga of Russia, became king of Greece. The third, Valdemar, chose for a wife Princess Marie of the royal house of Orleans.

* **Christian:** Christian IX, 1818–1906, king of Denmark and Norway.

The Writer's Craft

1. The topic sentence states that Christian's children made uncommonly good diplomatic marriages. Does the author include facts enough to establish the truth of that statement? How many does he give?

2. Would the topic sentence be convincing here if factual details had not been given to support it? Why, or why not?

Now You Try It

Choose one of the following topic sentences, or a topic sentence of your own, to develop in a brief, unified paragraph that contains supporting facts or examples.

a. Interplanetary travel is no longer a wild dream.
b. _____ is the most versatile person I know.
c. Many of our words are derived from the language of the American Indian.
d. Our school clubs span a wide variety of interests.
e. Waitresses have a vocabulary all their own.

DEVELOPMENT WITH AN INCIDENT Incidents may provide an effective means of illustrating the idea expressed in a topic sentence. In the following paragraph Christopher Morley makes a point by citing an incident from his childhood.

14   Christopher Morley in "Mince Pie"

Mothers are great in the eyes of their sons because they are knit in our minds with all the littlenesses of life, the unspeakably dear trifles and odds of existence. The other day I found in my desk a little strip of tape on which my name was marked a dozen times in drawing ink, in my mother's familiar script. My mind ran back to the time when that little band of humble linen was a kind of passport into manhood. It was when I went away from home and she could no longer mark my garments with my name, for the confusion of rapacious * laundries. I was to cut off the autographed sections of this tape and sew them on such new vestments as came my way. Of course I did not do so; what boy would be faithful to so feminine a trust? But now the little tape, soiled by a dozen years of wandering, lies in my desk drawer as a symbol and souvenir of that endless forethought and loving kindness.

* **rapacious:** grasping, greedy.

The Writer's Craft

1. What general statement does the author make in his topic sentence? How does the incident related in the paragraph help explain and illustrate the meaning of the general statement? Does the incident provide an effective and interesting way to develop the topic sentence? Why, or why not?

2. Why is it important for incidents used in the development of a paragraph to keep to the point? Is Morley's incident to the point or does it include unrelated details? Which details, if any, are unrelated?

Here is another paragraph in which the writer uses an incident to support his main idea.

15   Raymond Schuessler
in "The Scourge of Noise"

We never completely adjust our physical, mental, or nervous mechanism to noise. No matter how familiar a repeated sound becomes, it never passes unheard. Even when asleep we hear sounds entering our bedrooms, for they register on our minds and cause unnecessary mental activity. During the war a soldier got so accustomed to artillery fire at three o'clock every morning that he slept right through the barrage. One morning the guns were still, the battlefield silent. Promptly at three o'clock the soldier awoke, jumped up, and shouted, "What was that!"

The Writer's Craft

1. What is the main idea of this paragraph? Does the incident about the soldier prove the author's point? Why, or why not?

2. Notice that Morley in Model 14 and Schuessler in this model both state the main idea of their paragraphs before relating the incidents. Of course a writer is not obliged always to follow that pattern. What are the advantages of doing so? What would be the effect of beginning with the incident and ending with the main idea that it illustrates?

Now You Try It

Using an incident, develop one of the following topic sentences, or a topic sentence of your own, in a brief paragraph.

a. Teachers often teach a good deal more than their subjects.
b. _____ sometimes seems human. (Name a pet.)
c. A football game on a rainy day is a miserable experience.
d. Sometimes a loser gains more than a winner.
e. First impressions are frequently misleading.
f. Practice doesn't always make perfect.

DEVELOPMENT WITH REASONS   Topic sentences often make statements that provoke the question "Why?" — "Why is this true?" or "Why do you say that?" In general, a writer who starts with such a statement should satisfy the reader's curiosity by giving reasons to support it. The reasons may consist of examples, incidents, or specific supporting opinions. Notice that E. B. White develops the following paragraph by giving reasons to support his opening statement.

16   E. B. White in *Here Is New York*

It is a miracle that New York works at all. The whole thing is implausible. Every time the residents brush their teeth, millions of gallons of water must be drawn from the Catskills and the hills of Westchester. When a young man in Manhattan writes a letter to his girl in Brooklyn, the love message gets blown to her through a pneumatic tube — *pfft* — just like that. The subterranean system of telephone cables, power lines, steam pipes, gas mains, and sewer pipes is reason enough to abandon the island to the gods and the weevils. Every time an incision is made in the pavement, the noisy surgeons expose ganglia that are tangled beyond belief. By rights New York should have destroyed itself long ago, from panic or fire or rioting or failure of some vital supply line in its circulatory system or from some deep labyrinthine short circuit. Long ago the city should have experienced an insoluble traffic snarl at some impossible bottleneck. It should have perished of hunger when food lines failed for a few days. It should have been wiped out by a plague starting in its slums or carried in by ships' rats. It should have been overwhelmed by the sea that licks at it on every side. The workers in its myriad cells should have succumbed to nerves, from the fearful pall of smoke-fog that drifts over every few days from Jersey, blotting out all light at noon and leaving the high offices suspended, men groping and depressed, and the sense of world's end. It should have been touched in the head by the August heat and gone off its rocker.

1. What opinion does White state in the topic sentence? Why does that kind of statement require support with reasons?

2. The author gives at least eight reasons to support his initial statement of opinion about New York. What are they? Was it necessary to give so many? If not, why do you think he included them all?

In the following paragraph William O. Douglas gives reasons for an opinion he holds about flying in the Himalayan mountains.

17 William O. Douglas in *Beyond the High Himalayas*

Flying the Himalayas is a difficult and hazardous enterprise. There are no weather reports for the pilots. The weather report mostly needed is a report on the few passes through which the plane must pass. These are passes deep in the range, remote from any trail or road, far removed from any lookout. The mountains from a distance may appear to be clear of fog and mist. Weather, however, makes up strong and fast in the Himalayas. The condensation over glaciers and snow fields often comes quickly and in a matter of minutes erases a peak. Every flight is an experimental journey. There are almost always some clouds over the mountains. The pilot gains the necessary altitude and then looks for the hole in the clouds that will carry him through. Often he has to turn back. There are times when it is easy to return. There are points beyond which there is no return. Maneuverability of small planes at high altitudes is not great because their ceiling is low. One who flies the Himalayas has perhaps a thousand-foot clearance beneath him; and sometimes he has less than a quarter of a mile on either side for turning. When he is in those spots he must go forward. That is why there is tenseness in the cockpit as the pilot feels his way along the cloud banks that border the high peaks and tries to make up his mind whether to go ahead or turn back.

The Writer's Craft

1. What opinion does the topic sentence express? Does the author give enough reasons in the rest of the paragraph to establish the soundness of that opinion? Explain.

2. In developing the paragraph Douglas might have related an incident illustrating the difficulties one pilot had in crossing the Himalayas. Explain why that method would not have been as effective as the one actually used to develop the paragraph.

Now You Try It

Write a brief paragraph giving reasons to support one of the topic sentences listed below or a topic sentence of your own.

a. We need more discipline in our society.
b. _____ is the greatest living actor.
c. A woman should be elected President of the United States.
d. _____ is a book for anyone who likes to laugh.
e. Appearances are often deceiving.
f. Putting on a school play is exhausting.
g. _____ is the best player in professional football.
h. _____ is (would be) a depressing place to live.

00192

LESSON **4**

Organization of Details

Sentences within a paragraph must be organized clearly and logically if they are to be effective. Of course, any number of organizational patterns may be utilized, varying from paragraph to paragraph to suit the writer's purpose and the nature of the details he includes. Patterns also vary in different types of paragraphs. This lesson examines some of the methods of organization used in descriptive, narrative, and expository paragraphs.

ORDER OF LOCATION IN DESCRIPTION   A descriptive paragraph inevitably includes details, and often the reader needs to know where those details are located in relation to each other. In such cases the writer presents them in some kind of order. Sometimes the order follows a clear pattern: perhaps from near to far, right to left, or top to bottom. More often, however, the order is less rigid, simply conveying the relation of one detail to another and presenting each detail in a way that makes its location obvious. Observe how the following descriptive paragraph clarifies the location of the details it mentions.

18   F. H. Smith in *The Fortunes of Oliver Horn*

Below him, bounding from rock to rock, ran the brook, laughing in the sunlight and tossing the spray high in the air in a mad frolic. Across this swirling line of silver lay a sparse meadow strewn with rock, plotted with squares of last year's crops — potatoes, string beans, and cabbages — and now combed into straight green lines of early buckwheat and turnips. Beyond this a ragged pasture, fenced with blackened stumps, from which came the tinkle of cow bells, and farther on the grim, silent forest — miles and miles of forest seamed by a single road leading to Moose Hillock and the Great Stone Face.

The Writer's Craft

1. The phrase *below him* in the first sentence indicates that the scene described is being viewed from above. The first detail mentioned is the brook, immediately below and closest to the viewer. The next detail mentioned is the meadow, evidently just beyond the brook. Where in this scene are the following details located: the ragged pasture, the black-stump fence, the forest, and the road?

2. The writer of the paragraph has presented details in a recognizable order, beginning with the closest and ending with the one farthest away. How does presenting the details in that order help you visualize the scene? Can you suggest other orders that the writer might have followed?

Here is another description, this time of a moving object. Details within the paragraph are presented in an order that creates an impression of motion.

19 Joseph Husband in *America at Work*

Every night at exactly eight minutes past nine, the limited roars through the village. I can see it coming several miles away, its powerful headlight fingering rails and telegraph wires with a shimmer of light. Silently and slowly it seems to draw nearer; then suddenly, it is almost above me. A wild roar of steam and driving wheels, the wail of its hoarse whistle at the crossing, and then, looming black against the night sky, it smashes past, and in the swing of drivers and connecting rods I think of a greyhound or a racehorse thundering the final stretch. High in the cab window, a motionless figure peers ahead into the night; suddenly he is blackly silhouetted by the glare of the opened fire door, and in the orange light I can see the fireman swing back and forth as he feeds his fire. The light burns against the flying steam and smoke above; then blackness — and now the white windows of the Pullmans flicker past, and through the swirl of dust and smoke I watch the two red lights sink down the track.

The Writer's Craft

1. The paragraph describes a moving train. The first detail mentioned is the train's headlight as the writer sees it approaching in the distance. What detail is mentioned last? In what order are all the details in the paragraph presented?

2. Of course the author was not writing this description as the train was passing by. Rather, he was describing it from memory, and could therefore have mentioned the details at random — skipping from the front to the rear and back again. If he had used such a random order, would you have received a vivid impression of a moving train? Why, or why not?

Now You Try It

Select one of the following assignments:

1. Imagine that you are viewing a scene from a fixed position; for example, you might be looking out the window of your kitchen, your schoolroom, or your dentist's office. Then write a paragraph describing what you see, including only those details that create a strong impression. Present what you include in a near-to-far order.

2. Write a paragraph describing a car or bus as it approaches and then passes you while you are standing still. First mention the details you see and hear as it approaches, next the details you are aware of as it passes, and finally those you view as it moves off in the distance.

CHRONOLOGICAL ORDER IN NARRATION Narratives, or stories, are composed of events that take place in a time sequence. Usually the writer presents the events in the order in which they occurred — that is, in *chronological order*. In reading the narrative paragraph below, about an incident in the Far West in the 1840's, notice the order in which the events are presented.

20   Francis Parkman in *The Oregon Trail*

The Panther, on his black-and-white horse, one of the best in the village, came at full speed over the hill in hot pursuit of an antelope, that darted away like lightning before him. The attempt was made in mere sport and bravado, for very few are the horses that can for a moment compete in swiftness with this little animal. The antelope ran down the hill towards the main body of the Indians, who were moving over the plain below. Sharp yells were given, and horsemen galloped out to intercept his flight. At this he turned sharply to the left, and scoured away with such speed that he distanced all his pursuers, even the vaunted horse of The Panther himself. A few moments after, we witnessed a more serious sport. A shaggy buffalo-bull bounded out from a neighboring hollow, and close behind him came a slender Indian boy, riding without stirrups or saddle, and lashing his eager little horse to full speed. Yard after yard he drew closer to his gigantic victim, though the bull, with his short tail erect and his tongue lolling out a foot from his foaming jaws, was straining his unwieldy strength to the utmost. A moment more, and the boy was close alongside. It was our friend the Hail-Storm. He dropped the rein on his horse's neck, and jerked an arrow like lightning from the quiver at his shoulder.

The Writer's Craft

1. The events in the paragraph are presented in chronological order. How do you know that the hunting of the buffalo-bull follows the pursuit of the antelope by the Indian called Panther?

Would any other organization of this paragraph have been as effective as the one used?

2. A chronological presentation of events organizes the details of a narrative paragraph effectively. Does it make clear the relationship between events? Does it allow the author to build to a climax? Explain.

Now You Try It

Write a brief narrative paragraph about an experience — real or imagined — but try to choose one that has a point to it. Present the separate events in chronological order and bring the story to a definite conclusion at the end of the paragraph.

CHRONOLOGICAL ORDER IN EXPOSITION Exposition is often used to give directions or explain a process. In such cases the details, or steps, are presented in chronological order. The details of the following paragraph, explaining how to get into a canoe, are organized chronologically.

21 Raymond R. Camp
in *The Young Sportsman's Guide to Canoeing*

An important technique to learn first is how to enter the canoe. This craft, with the stern resting on the shore and the bow in the water, is in its most unstable position. The stern paddler first steadies the canoe. He places one foot on either side of the stern, pressing with his knees to hold it firmly. Then he grasps either gunwale * with his hands, approximately eighteen inches forward. The bow paddler then steps to the center of the canoe just forward of the stern seat with one foot, grasps the gunwale while he brings in the other foot, then moves forward, bent at right angles from the waist. Sliding his hands forward on either gunwale, he moves to the bow seat. His hands do not leave the gunwales until he is seated. He then sits *immovable* while the stern paddler places one foot into the canoe just forward of his seat, grasps the gunwales,

* **gunwale:** top edge of a canoe.

and thrusts the canoe gently out into the water with the other leg. With the canoe in motion he brings his other leg into the canoe. If this seems time-consuming and silly to you, watch a pair of northwoods voyageurs who have spent their lives in a canoe. You will find that they follow this procedure automatically, not because the book says so, but because they have learned through experience that this is the easiest and safest method.

The Writer's Craft

1. The paragraph conveys instructions clearly. They would not have been clear, however, if the various steps had been presented in some other order. Explain why chronological order is essential in paragraphs explaining how to do something.

2. Chronological order alone, of course, is not all that is required to make instruction clear. Each step must be described precisely. The author of Model 21 begins his explanation with the following sentences:

> The stern paddler first steadies the canoe. He places one foot on either side of the stern, pressing with his knees to hold it firmly. Then he grasps either gunwale with his hands, approximately eighteen inches forward.

Suppose he had written instead:

> Someone steadies the canoe by holding on to both sides of the stern with his knees and hands.

Why is this second version inferior to the original?

Now You Try It

Write a paragraph explaining how to do something. Be sure to give precise instructions and to present the steps in chronological order. The following topics may be helpful as suggestions.

a. How to give artificial respiration
b. How to get from school to your house
c. How to start a car
d. How to dive
e. How to serve a tennis ball

ORDER OF IMPORTANCE IN EXPOSITION   Sometimes details in a paragraph may differ in scope or degree. That is, one detail may have broader application or deeper significance than the others. In such instances common sense suggests that the organization of the paragraph reflect that difference. In other words, the broadest or most important detail should be placed either first or last in the paragraph. In the following example the humorist James Thurber, voicing an opinion about women, presents his supporting details in an order that reflects their importance.

22   James Thurber in "The Case Against Women"

I (to quit hiding behind the generalization of "the male") hate women because they almost never get anything right. They say, "I have been faithful to thee, Cynara, after my fashion" instead of "in my fashion." They will bet you that Alfred Smith's middle name is Aloysius, instead of Emanuel. They will tell you to take the 2:57 train, on a day that the 2:57 does not run, or, if it does run, does not stop at the station where you are supposed to get off. Many men, separated from a woman by this particular form of imprecision, have never showed up in her life again. Nothing so embitters a man as to end up in Bridgeport, when he was supposed to get off at Westport.

The Writer's Craft

1. In his topic sentence Thurber maintains that he hates women because they almost never get anything right. He develops the paragraph by giving three typical examples of women's inability to get details right. What are the examples?

2. Is the most serious error given first or last? Is the order in which the examples are presented effective? Why, or why not?

Now You Try It

Write a paragraph developing one of the topic sentences suggested below, or one of your own choice. Present supporting details in the order of their importance, beginning with the least and ending with the most important detail. Place the topic sentence at the beginning of the paragraph.

a. I like _____ movies best. (Name the kind.)
b. The voting age should be lowered to eighteen across the nation.
c. In general, speed limits on interstate highways are set too high.
d. Students should have the right to determine what courses they take in high school.
e. The benefits of a regular program of athletics are many.
f. I like old houses better than new ones.

ORDER IN A PARAGRAPH OF COMPARISON OR CONTRAST
Paragraphs developed by *comparisons* (which show similarities) or by *contrasts* (which show differences) require a special pattern of organization. One of the two organizational patterns possible is illustrated in the paragraph below.

23 John S. Terry
in *Thomas Wolfe's Letters to His Mother*

The heads of mother and son showed little physical resemblance. Mrs. Wolfe had a delicate-boned face and fair, thin skin which was as delicate as ivory. Her nose was small with a strong, but not prominent bridge, and was rounded at the end. Her small cheekbones just broke the flatness of her wide, round face. Tom's olive-complexioned face was large and unusually pale; his brow was massive, his nose long but not well formed, for it too had a smaller bridge than one would have expected. His black hair was always unruly, and since he seldom took time to get it cut, his great head often resembled, in its titanic nobility and volume, the Bourdelle * bust of Beethoven. His large brown eyes dominated all his other features, and often in moments of deep thought he would close them, almost as if to cut off the outside world, and to hide what he was undergoing.

* **Bourdelle:** a twentieth-century French sculptor.

1. Which is the topic sentence in this paragraph? Does it indicate that the writer is going to show similarities or differences?

2. The writer develops his paragraph by comparing the heads of a mother and her son. First he presents all the details about one, then all the details about the other. Such an organization creates a separate total impression of each of the two things being compared. What general impression do you have of Mrs. Wolfe's head? of Thomas Wolfe's?

3. Alternatively, a paragraph of comparison or contrast may be organized by comparing or contrasting individual features. If the author of Model 23 had used that method, he would have paired the individual points of contrast between Thomas Wolfe's and his mother's heads:

> The heads of mother and son showed little physical resemblance. Mrs. Wolfe's skin was a delicate ivory, while Tom's complexion was olive. She had a small nose and Tom had a long nose. Her face was delicate and flat; Tom's was large and he had a massive brow.

Why would such a point-by-point pattern have been a less satisfactory way to organize Model 23 than the pattern Terry used?

Now You Try It

From the subjects below, select a pair to use as the basis for a short paragraph of comparison or contrast. If you prefer, choose two subjects of your own.

a. You and your brother (or sister)
b. Thinking and doing
c. City life and country life
d. Work and play
e. Youth and age
f. Watching television and reading a book

Before beginning the paragraph, jot down details that you plan to include about each subject. Decide whether it would be more effective to create a total impression of each of the subjects being compared, or to make a point-by-point comparison between them. Organize your details accordingly.

LESSON **5**

Coherence in Paragraphs

To be effective, a paragraph must be coherent. That is, sentences within the paragraph must be linked so that thoughts being expressed move smoothly from one sentence to the next. Coherence is achieved in two ways: by presenting sentences in a logical order, and by using words and phrases that make the relationship between them clear. This lesson examines some of the ways writers help their readers understand the connection between sentences. It should be noted that although the lesson necessarily presents the devices used one at a time, all of them frequently work together in making a paragraph coherent.

COHERENCE THROUGH THE USE OF PRONOUNS Once a subject has been named, pronouns are particularly helpful as linking expressions. In reading the following paragraph, notice how the underscored pronouns help give it coherence.

24   W. Maxwell Reed in *America's Treasure*

While the earth was growing, and perhaps before that time, some unusually heavy atoms were formed. One group is the substance we call uranium. These atoms are so large and complex that they are unstable, which means in this case that they will explode. Why they should do this we do not know. We   5 all know why gunpowder explodes. It is perfectly stable until something, the atoms of which are moving with tremendous speed, comes in contact with it. A spark or a red-hot iron will prove to anyone that 10 gunpowder is unstable. A piece of uranium contains so many thousands of millions of atoms that some can be exploding all the time and yet the piece of uranium will grow smaller and lighter with great slowness. Fortunately uranium breaks up in this way 15 at a certain definite rate. So when rock containing bits of uranium is found, chemists can tell how many millions of years ago that rock was formed.

The Writer's Craft

1. Pronouns can refer either to elements in an earlier part of the same sentence or to elements in a preceding sentence. To what do the following pronouns in the paragraph refer?

they (lines 4, 5 and 6)
this (line 6)
it (lines 7 and 9)

2. Several underscored pronouns in the passage are used as adjectives to modify nouns. So used, they indicate that the noun they modify refers to an element mentioned previously. In line 2, "that time" refers back to the time when the earth was growing, mentioned at the beginning of the sentence. Find the element referred to by each of the following:

These atoms (lines 3–4)
this way (line 15)
that rock (line 18)

COHERENCE THROUGH TRANSITIONAL EXPRESSIONS   Such words and phrases as *however, therefore, in addition, on the other hand, then,* and *meanwhile* help show the relationship between ideas in a paragraph. As you read the following paragraphs, observe how the underscored *transitional expressions* — as those words and phrases are called — provide a link between sentences.

25   Edmund Callis Berkeley in *Giant Brains*

A machine can handle information; it can calculate, conclude, and choose; it can perform reasonable operations with information. A machine, therefore, can think. Now when we speak of a machine that thinks, or a mechanical brain, what do we mean? Essentially, a mechanical brain is a machine that handles information, transfers information automatically from one part of the machine to another, and has a flexible control over the sequence of its operations. No human being is needed around such a machine to pick up a physical piece of information produced in one part of the machine, personally move it to another part of the machine, and there put it in again. Nor is any human being needed to give the machine instructions from minute to minute. Instead, we can write out the whole program to solve a problem, translate the program into machine language, and put the program into the machine. Then we press the start button; the machine starts whirring; and it prints out the answers as it obtains them.

26   Alfred Werner in "The Most Mysterious Manuscript"

Cryptography, the "act or art of writing in secret characters," is mentioned by Roman authors of the first century A.D. as having been used in the time of Julius Caesar, but undoubtedly it dates back much further in origin. For there have always been nonconformists * and heretics ° who had something important to say but could not, or would not, run the risk of having their message read by secular or religious authorities for fear of persecution. Yet these thinkers did not wish to keep their ideas or their knowledge entirely to them-

---

* **nonconformists:** people who oppose the rules and regulations of society or of a particular institution.
° **heretics:** people who hold beliefs contrary to the established doctrines of a religious system.

selves. Hence it was only logical to devise a code so that they could make their statements in a language that, to the ordinary eye, would cause the manuscript to appear to be the meaningless work of a crank. The author, however, would take steps to make sure that this "subversive" text could be understood by posterity; he might confide the key to unraveling the script to a trustworthy young disciple, or he might — often at the end of the manuscript — insert the key in such a way that it would reveal itself to an earnest student willing to devote countless hours to the task of decipherment.

The Writer's Craft

1. Here are some of the more commonly used transitional expressions and the purposes they fulfill.

> *Adding an idea or fact:* also, another, besides, furthermore, moreover, in addition, again, second, third, finally, next, too, similarly
>
> *Establishing time order:* first, then, next, meanwhile, before, after, finally, later
>
> *Showing a cause-and-effect relationship:* as a result, consequently, hence, therefore, thus, accordingly
>
> *Indicating an illustration:* for example, for instance
>
> *Indicating a contrast, contradiction, or restriction:* however, nevertheless, on the contrary, on the other hand, yet, otherwise
>
> *Showing a comparison:* similarly, likewise
>
> *Establishing a spatial order:* above, below, here, there, inside, outside, nearby, beyond, over, under

In Models 25 and 26 what purpose does each of the transitional expressions serve? In other words, what relationship between ideas does each expression indicate?

2. A transitional expression should be used whenever there is a likelihood that a relationship between ideas will not be clear without it. Would it be possible to omit any of the transitional expressions in either model? Try removing each one of them and explain the effect on the paragraph.

Still another way of achieving coherence is through the repetition of key words. The following paragraph achieves coherence partly by that means.

27 Stephen Leacock in "Oxford as I See It"

In spite of its dilapidated buildings and its lack of fire escapes, ventilation, sanitation, and up-to-date kitchen facilities, I persist in my assertion that Oxford, in its way, is the greatest university in the world. I am aware that this is an extreme statement and needs explanation. Oxford is much smaller in numbers, for example, than the State University of Minnesota, and is much poorer. It has, or had till yesterday, fewer students than the University of Toronto. To mention Oxford beside the 26,000 students of Columbia University sounds ridiculous. In point of money, the $39,000,-000 endowment of the University of Chicago, and the $35,000,000 one of Columbia, and the $43,000,000 of Harvard seem to leave Oxford nowhere. Yet the peculiar thing is that it is not nowhere. By some queer process of its own it seems to get there every time. It was therefore of the very greatest interest to me, as a profound scholar, to try to investigate just how this peculiar excellence of Oxford arises.

The Writer's Craft

1. The key word in this paragraph, which compares one university with others, is *Oxford*. How does repeating *Oxford* help make the paragraph coherent? To answer the question, compare the original with the rewritten version below, in which the pronoun *it* has been substituted for the repetitions of *Oxford*.

> In spite of its dilapidated buildings and its lack of fire escapes, ventilation, sanitation, and up-to-date kitchen facilities, I persist in my assertion that Oxford, in its way, is the greatest university in the world. I am aware that this is an extreme statement and needs explanation. It is much

smaller in numbers, for example, than the State University of Minnesota, and is much poorer. It has, or had till yesterday, fewer students than the University of Toronto. To mention _it_ beside the 26,000 students of Columbia University sounds ridiculous. In point of money, the $39,000,-000 endowment of the University of Chicago, and the $35,000,000 one of Columbia, and the $43,000,000 of Harvard seem to leave _it_ nowhere. Yet the peculiar thing is that it is not nowhere. By some queer process of its own it seems to get there every time. It was therefore of the very greatest interest to me, as a profound scholar, to try to investigate just how _its_ peculiar excellence arises.

Why is it better to use _Oxford_ in the four places in the paragraph where _it_ or _its_ has been underscored?

2. In addition to repeating _Oxford,_ the author uses transitional expressions to achieve coherence. Find three transitional expressions in the model and explain their function.

Now You Try It

Select one of the following topic sentences and use specific details to develop it into a paragraph. Wherever necessary, include transitional expressions, pronouns, and repetition to give the paragraph coherence. Underscore the transitional expressions you use.

a. A sensible person budgets his time.
b. It is ridiculous to believe that _____. (Name a popular superstition.)
c. Our town should set up a youth center.
d. Carelessness often causes serious accidents.
e. Raising puppies is as much work as pleasure.
f. It is easy to take good photographs if you follow a few basic rules.
g. Fads in children's toys quickly come and go.
h. Today, as in the past, men are pushing beyond new frontiers.

Description

LESSON **6**

Skills of Descriptive Writing

Descriptive writing seeks to create a clear picture or impression of a person, place, or object. It grows out of a writer's ability to observe closely, then through skillful use of words to convey those observations in writing. As an example, the model in this lesson, which describes an old sailing ship preparing to leave harbor, employs many of the skills that make descriptive writing effective.

28   John J. Floherty in *Search and Rescue at Sea*

The November wind, whistling down from the north, was flecked with Arctic snow. Dun-gray clouds rolled across the dreary Newfoundland landscape. Dark patches of open water showed here and there in the threadbare blanket of ice that covered ⁵ the harbor. A winter haze dimmed the distant headland that gave a semblance of protection to shipping. In the ramshackle dock the three-masted schooner *Maria Carlotta* huddled close to the wharf, cringing under the whip of the weather. ¹⁰

As a vessel, she was not much to look at. Seascarred, unpainted, her shabbiness was relieved by the orderly appearance of her deck gear. Halyards and lifts and sheets were coiled neatly on their respective pins. On her afterdeck her wheel of teak ¹⁵ freshly varnished, her brass binnacle * freshly

* **binnacle:** a stand for a ship's compass.

shined, sparkled in the watery light. For all her poverty-stricken appearance, it was evident that in her heyday — say thirty years ago — she could hold her head as high as any in the great fleet of fore-and- 20 afters that carried much of our coastwise commerce. The sweet lines of her hull were born on the drafting board of a master designer. From the curving stem and hollow lines of her bow, she might well have been kin to the *Flying Cloud,* the *Shenandoah,* 25 and the other famous clippers that gave America supremacy on the Seven Seas half a century before she was built.

With cargo stowed and hatches battened down, the crew under the sharp eye of the mate were en- 30 gaged in a dozen duties preparatory to sailing. Boat gripes were secured, gaskets cast off, headsails were bent, brooms were swishing the deck clear of debris accumulated during the loading. From "Charley Noble," the soot-stained stack on the galley, a pennant 35 of smoke drifted to leeward while an aura of fish chowder seeped through the schooner. Soon after high water a decrepit tug wheezed into the dock. It was sailing time. Breastlines were cast off, a hawser was passed to the tug, huffing and puffing under the 40 schooner's bow. A prolonged whistle blast, a churning of muddy water, and the voyage to Lisbon had begun with high hopes of fair weather and a good landfall.

The Writer's Craft

SELECTING DETAILS AND MAKING THEM SPECIFIC

In describing something, the writer first decides which details to mention and which to omit. Only significant details, frequently those that help create a particular impression, are included. The writer then makes each detail as specific and vivid as possible.

This description of an old schooner preparing to set sail depicts three aspects of the scene: the setting, the appearance of the ship, and the activity on board and in the harbor. Consider the description of the setting in the first paragraph. Included are details of the wind, clouds, water and ice in the harbor, the dock, and the schooner. Each detail is made specific. The wind, for example, is specified as *whistling down from the north* and being *flecked with Arctic snow*. The picture of the clouds is made more specific by the author's noting that they were *dun-gray*. How are the rest of the details in the paragraph made specific? In other words, what information is given about the water, the ice, the dock, and the schooner?

The second paragraph includes two general statements about the ship's appearance. For one thing, "she was not much to look at." What details have been selected to support that statement? But even though she had a poverty-stricken appearance, we learn in the middle of the paragraph that she had once been a fine ship. What sentence contains that general statement? What details support the statement? How are those details made specific?

The final paragraph contains details selected to show the activity on board ship and in the harbor. What details have been included? How have they been made specific?

USING SENSORY DETAILS

Details in descriptive writing appeal to the senses. Very often the writer chooses to mention details of appearance, but details of sound, smell, touch, and taste also help create a total impression of whatever is being described. The selection above appeals primarily to the sense of sight, inasmuch as many of the details describe the ship's appearance. What words or phrases help you see the following parts of the ship?

the halyards, lifts, and sheets (lines 13–15)
the wheel and the brass binnacle (lines 15–17)
the stack (lines 34–35)

In addition, the selection does appeal briefly to the senses of hearing and smell. The earliest appeal to the sense of hearing occurs in the first line, where the wind is described as "whistling down from the north." In what ways do lines 33, 38, and 40–41 appeal to the sense of hearing? What detail in lines 36–37 appeals to the sense of smell?

ARRANGING DETAILS

The details of a description should be arranged effectively. In this selection, related details are grouped together in separate paragraphs. As has been noted, the first paragraph provides details of setting; the second furnishes details of the ship's appearance; and the third gives details of activity on and around the ship. Is this an effective pattern for organizing the selection? Could the writer have presented his details in any other order? If so, explain what that order might have been.

CHOOSING WORDS

Only through the use of precise nouns and verbs and vivid adjectives and adverbs can the writer evoke a clear picture of the person, place, or object he is describing. Consider the precise verbs in this selection. The first paragraph is reprinted below. After rereading it, explain why the verbs in boldface are particularly effective.

> The November wind, whistling down from the north, **was flecked** with Arctic snow. Dun-gray clouds **rolled** across the dreary Newfoundland landscape. Dark patches of open water showed here and there in the threadbare blanket of ice that covered the harbor. A winter haze **dimmed** the distant headland that gave a semblance of protection to shipping. In the ramshackle dock the three-masted schooner *Maria Carlotta* **huddled** close to the wharf, cringing under the whip of the weather.

Point out at least three precise verbs in both the second and third paragraphs of the selection.

Now You Try It

Following the example of the model, write a description of a scene in which a vehicle is the principal object. Suggestions might include a train in a station, a plane before takeoff, a sailboat leaving its buoy, a truck being loaded, a cart from which vegetables are being sold at the side of a road, a space capsule on its launching pad or in the sea after re-entry, or a sports car at the start of a race. Write at least two paragraphs, devoting one to each aspect of the scene. If you wish to follow the organization of the model, describe the setting in the first paragraph, the appearance of the vehicle in the second, and the activity on and around the vehicle in the third; but if some other organization seems preferable, by all means use it. Be sure that your finished description is not only well-organized but vivid, and remember to select your details carefully and use precise words.

LESSON **7**

Selecting Details

Not every detail of a person, object, or scene should be included in a description. On the contrary, from all the details present the writer carefully selects only a few — those that will contribute to the purpose of the description. The two models in this lesson illustrate details selected for slightly different purposes. In one, they help support a general statement; in the other, they help convey a strong, unified impression to the reader.

SUPPORTING A GENERAL STATEMENT   The model below describes October. Notice how the opening general statement is related to the descriptive, sensory details that follow it.

29   Thomas Wolfe in *Of Time and the River*

October is the richest of the seasons. The fields are cut, the granaries are full, the bins are loaded to the brim with fatness, and from the cider press the rich brown oozings of the York Imperials run. The bee bores to the belly of the yellowed grape, the fly ⁵ gets old and fat and blue, he buzzes loud, crawls slow, creeps heavily to death on sill and ceiling, the sun goes down in blood and pollen across the bronzed and mown fields of old October.

The corn is shocked: it sticks out in hard yellow [10] rows upon dried ears, fit now for great red barns in Pennsylvania and the bit-stained teeth of crunching horses. The indolent hooves kick swiftly at the boards, the barn is sweet with hay and leather, wood and apples — *this,* and the clean dry crunching of [15] the teeth is all: the sweat, the labor, and the plow is over. The late pears mellow on a sunny shelf; smoked hams hang to the warped barn rafters; the pantry shelves are loaded with 300 jars of fruit. Meanwhile the leaves are turning, turning, up in [20] Maine, the chestnut burrs plop thickly to the earth in gusts of wind, and in Virginia the chinkapins are falling.

There is a smell of burning in small towns in after-noon, and men with buckles on their arms are rak- [25] ing leaves in yards as boys come by with straps slung back across their shoulders. The oak leaves, big and brown, are bedded deep in yard and gutter: they make deep wadings to the knee for children in the streets. The fire will snap and crackle like a [30] whip, sharp acrid smoke will sting the eyes, in mown fields the little vipers of the flame eat past the black coarse edges of burned stubble like a line of locusts. Fire drives a thorn of memory in the heart.

The Writer's Craft

1. The first sentence states an overall impression of October. What general statement does the sentence make?

2. Details in the three paragraphs were selected to support the general statement that October is the richest of the seasons. In each paragraph find three details that seem especially effective in conveying an impression of richness. Should any details have been omitted? If so, explain why.

3. Notice that an impression of the month is evoked by details that appeal not only to the sense of sight but also to the senses of hearing, taste, and smell. To which sense or senses does each of the details in the three paragraphs appeal?

In composing a description, a writer chooses words and phrases that create vivid sensory impressions. Explain why the italicized words in the following extracts from the model are especially effective choices:

> . . . from the cider press the rich brown *oozings* of the York Imperials run.
>
> The bee *bores* to the *belly* of the yellowed grape . . .
>
> . . . the sun goes down in *blood and pollen* across the *bronzed* and mown fields of old October.
>
> . . . the barn is *sweet* with hay and leather, wood and apples . . .
>
> The late pears *mellow* on a sunny shelf . . .
>
> . . . the chestnut burrs *plop* thickly to the earth . . .
>
> The fire will *snap* and *crackle* . . .

Can you think of any words to substitute for the italicized words in order to produce even more vivid impressions? If so, what are they?

FIGURATIVE LANGUAGE: METAPHORS AND SIMILES

In descriptive writing — as in other kinds of prose and poetry — forceful images may be created by comparing two fundamentally different things on the basis of a characteristic they have in common. A book and a jungle are quite different commodities, but a writer might describe a particularly tedious book by comparing the two: "Getting through that book was like hacking a path through the densest jungle." The comparison makes for a more vivid picture than would have been evoked if the writer had said simply: "The book was hard to read."

The comparison in the sentence, "Getting through that book was like hacking a path through the densest jungle," is called a *simile;* notice that it uses the word *like* in comparing the two dissimilar objects. Invariably, similes make use of *like, as,* or *than.* The following are two similes from Wolfe's description of October:

> The fire will snap and crackle *like* a whip . . .
>
> . . . the little vipers of the flame eat past the black coarse edges of burned stubble *like a line of locusts.*

Read the extracts without the italicized comparisons. Do you hear the sound of the fire as clearly? Do you have as vivid a picture of the movement of the fire? Explain.

Metaphors are comparisons that do not use *like, as,* or *than,* but simply present one thing as another: "The reader must hack his way through a jungle of tangled words and twisted thoughts"; "Her smile was sunshine on a rainy day"; "My hopes are armor against discouragement." Several metaphors occur in the selection. Line 32, for example, mentions *the little vipers of the flame* eating past the black coarse edges of burned stubble. The italicized phrase is a metaphor, comparing the flame to little vipers, or poisonous snakes, and thereby suggesting that the flames are quick-moving and destructive. The last sentence in the selection, "Fire drives a thorn of memory in the heart," includes another metaphor. By comparing the effect of the fire to that of a thorn driven into the heart, the author creates a forceful image of the emotional reaction one has to the sight and smell of October's fires.

Now You Try It

Consider your reactions to the different months of the year (excluding October). Which one creates a particularly strong impression? Write one or two paragraphs describing that month, beginning, like Thomas Wolfe, with a general statement of the impression in the first sentence. Then develop the composition with details that create a similar impression for your readers. Select details that appeal not only to the sense of sight, but to the senses of hearing, taste, touch, and smell as well. Use precise words and comparisons to make details vivid. Exclude any details that do not contribute to the overall impression.

CREATING AN IMPRESSION A description of a person is frequently intended to create a clear impression of outstanding traits or characteristics. Accordingly, the writer selects only those details of the person's appearance and behavior that will contribute to that impression. As you read the following description, notice how Dickens creates a distinct impression of the wineshop keeper.

The wineshop keeper was a bull-necked, martial-looking man of thirty, and he should have been of a hot temperament, for, although it was a bitter day, he wore no coat, but carried one slung over his shoulder. His shirt sleeves were rolled up, too, and his brown arms were bare to the elbows. Neither did he wear anything more on his head than his own crisply curling short dark hair. He was a dark man altogether, with good eyes and a good bold breadth between them. Good-humored looking on the whole, but implacable looking, too; evidently a man of a strong resolution and a set purpose; a man not desirable to be met, rushing down a narrow pass with a gulf on either side, for nothing would turn the man.

The Writer's Craft

1. The wineshop keeper's outstanding trait is stated in the last sentence of the paragraph, which describes him as "a man of strong resolution and a set purpose" — a man whom "nothing would turn." In other words, he is determined and single-minded in his purposefulness. What details does the author mention before making that final statement? How do the details contribute to the impression created by the wineshop keeper and conveyed by the author in the course of the paragraph?

2. Let us assume that the writer of the paragraph below had the same man in mind that Dickens was describing. Notice that no details have been changed, but a few have been added and some omitted.

> The wineshop keeper was a man of thirty. He had a coat slung over his shoulders, and his white shirt sleeves were rolled up, revealing muscular arms. His crisply curling short dark hair sparkled in the sunlight. His eyes were good and his humor cheerful. A smile played across his lips. It was obvious that nothing would turn the man.

Do details in the first three sentences suggest that the wineshop keeper was a man whom "nothing would turn"? What details in this passage do not contribute to creating the impression of his determination? What details in Dickens's passage, but not in this rewritten version, contribute to that impression?

Now You Try It

Think of someone who has strongly impressed you, perhaps with his kindness or timidity or courage or stubbornness or good humor. Write a paragraph describing that person. If you wish, begin by stating your general impression of the person; or you may prefer to state your impression in the last sentence, as Dickens does. Select details of appearance, clothing, mannerisms, or any other characteristics related to the dominant impression that the person creates, and make the details you include as vivid as possible.

LESSON **8**

Using Sensory Details

As you have seen, descriptive writing creates an impression in part through sensory details, appealing to the reader's senses of sight, hearing, smell, taste, and touch. Sensory details in the following selection help create a vivid impression of the wonders of an old-fashioned circus parade.

31   Charles Philip Fox in *A Ticket to the Circus*

One of the most glorious and delightful aspects of the circus is now gone forever. In its heyday the parade's purpose was to advertise the show's presence in town and stir up excitement, interest, and enthusiasm in the people. And this it did — for no other ⁵ advertising medium ever devised so played upon the three key senses of man. For the eye there were the gigantic gold-leafed bandwagons pulled by ten-horse teams; scores of beautifully appointed ladies riding on sleek well-groomed horses; colorful ze- ¹⁰ bras; clowns riding donkey carts; haughty camels, and plodding elephants bedecked in gorgeous red velvet robes covered with sparkling spangles; glorious wood-carved tableaux representing faraway countries; open cages and dens of wild animals, col- ¹⁵ orful birds and reptiles from all over the world. For the ear there were many bands high up on wagons

and playing stirring circus music. There were bell
wagons, organs, and the shrieking, puffing, blowing
steam calliope.* Then there were special sounds ²⁰
that could only be heard in a circus parade . . . the
deep-throated knock of the heavy wheels caused by
the slight lateral motion of the wheel when it hit the
axle housing; the soft shuffling sound as dozens of
elephants slid their sandpaperlike feet on the pave- ²⁵
ment; the clopping of forty shod hooves as a ten-
horse hitch passed by; the rattle of chains on the
eveners; the sudden roar of a tiger or lion. Then,
too, the parade imparted to the nose very special
odors that added a thrilling touch of reality to the ³⁰
whole spectacular pageant — a fantastic array of
wild animals, each with its own peculiar jungle scent
drifting out from the cage; the individual exotic
aroma of the camels, not quite like a horse; and the
dense, penetrating odor of the elephants.   ³⁵

* **calliope:** a musical instrument consisting of a keyboard and a
series of steam whistles.

The Writer's Craft

1. The description contains details that enable the reader to
see, hear, and even smell the circus parade. Mention of the
bandwagons (line 8) appeals to the sense of sight. But if the
author had simply said that there were bandwagons in the parade, a sharp picture would not have been created in your mind.
To enable you to see the bandwagons clearly, he specifies that
they were "gigantic" and "gold-leafed" and that they were "pulled
by ten-horse teams." What words and phrases enable you to see
clearly the following aspects of the parade?

the ladies on horseback (lines 9–10)
the zebras (lines 10–11)
the clowns (line 11)
the elephants (lines 12–13)
the tableaux representing faraway countries (lines 13–15)

2. Having specified the sights, the author next describes some
of the sounds of the parade. What words and phrases let you

distinctly hear the sounds made by the parts of the parade listed below?

the bands (lines 17–18)
the calliope (lines 19–20)
the wagon wheels (lines 22–24)
the elephants (lines 24–26)
the ten-horse hitch (lines 26–27)
the chains (lines 27–28)
the tigers and lions (line 28)

3. The final sensory appeal is to the reader's sense of smell. What words and phrases describe the odors of the wild animals (lines 31–33)? the camels (lines 33–34)? the elephants (line 35)?

4. How are details arranged in this paragraph? Do you find the order effective? Why, or why not?

WORD CHOICE: APPEALING TO THE SENSES

1. To create vivid impressions, the writer must use words that evoke a strong sensory response in the reader's imagination. To judge the effectiveness of an author's choice of words, compare the pairs of phrases below. The first phrase in each pair is taken from the selection; the second is a rewritten version of the same phrase. For each pair explain why the original version is more effective than the rewritten one.

Original:
the shrieking, puffing, blowing steam calliope
Rewritten:
the very noisy steam calliope

Original:
the deep-throated knock of the heavy wheels
Rewritten:
the loud noise of the heavy wheels

Original:
the clopping of forty shod hooves
Rewritten:
the sound of forty shod hooves

Original:
the dense, penetrating odor of the elephants
Rewritten:
the strong odor of the elephants

2. What words might create a vivid sensory impression of the following details? For each item, give at least two adjectives or adjective phrases.

a. The sound of a car stopping
b. The taste of pepper
c. The smell of a river or the sea

The narrator of the following selection is traveling on horseback down a mountain with a friend. Notice the sensory details in this brief descriptive passage from a novel.

32 Walter Van Tilburg Clark in *The Ox-Bow Incident*

We reined to the right and went slowly down the steep stage road. It was a switchback road, gutted by the runoff of the winter storms, and with brush beginning to grow up in it again since the stage had stopped running. In the pockets under the red earth banks, where the wind was cut off, the spring sun was hot as summer, and the air was full of a hot melting pine smell. Rivulets of water trickled down shining on the sides of the cuts. The jays screeched in the trees and flashed through the sunlight in the clearings in swift, long dips. Squirrels and chipmunks chittered in the brush and along the tops of snow-sodden logs. On the outside turns, though, the wind got to us and dried the sweat under our shirts and brought up, instead of the hot resin, the smell of the marshy green valley. In the west the heads of a few clouds showed, the kind that come up with the early heat, but they were lying still, and over us the sky was clear and deep.

The Writer's Craft

Many sensory details are included in this selection. Find:

a. Three details that appeal to the sense of sight
b. Three that appeal to the sense of hearing
c. Three that appeal to the sense of smell

1. In description, as you know, carefully chosen verbs help create vivid impressions. Find at least four verbs in the selection that appeal vividly either to the sense of sight or to the sense of hearing.

2. Replace each of the italicized verbs in the following sentences with a verb more vividly descriptive. If you wish, suggest several possible replacements.

a. The man *talked* on and on.
b. The girls *laughed* at the joke.
c. The paste *came* out of the tube.
d. The steak *was cooking* on the grill.
e. The tiger *looked* through the bars.

Now You Try It

1. The following paragraph, which sets out to describe a squirrel in the yard on an autumn day, fails to create a vivid picture. Rewrite the paragraph, using vivid words and sensory details that make the description appeal to the imagination. Below the paragraph are questions that suggest ways to improve it.

> It was a nice autumn day. In the yard a squirrel ran in and out of the leaves. He made a lot of noise and seemed to be looking for something. Finally he found what he wanted and went up the tree. The squirrel's hiding place was visible through the branches.

a. Why is it a "nice" day?
b. What did the squirrel look like? What noises did he make?
c. What words would describe the appearance of the leaves and the squirrel's search through them?
d. What did the squirrel find? Should it be described?
e. What do you see as you look up through the branches at the squirrel's hiding place?

2. Write a description of a particular place at a specific time: for example, the school cafeteria at noon; the locker room before a game; a dance as it looks when you first arrive; a bus, train, or subway during rush hour; a department store during the Christmas season. Limiting your description to about 350 words, include details that appeal to at least three of the senses.

LESSON

Locating Details

Usually the reader needs to know where individual details that make up a scene are located, and how they are related to each other. To indicate location, a writer uses words and phrases that reveal spatial relationships — expressions such as *over, beneath, beside, on the right, between,* or *in the distance.* This lesson presents two models in which the location of details is important to the overall effect of the description. The first is written from a fixed or stationary vantage point; the second, from a moving vantage point.

A STATIONARY VANTAGE POINT   The following description relates what a man experienced as he sat inside a cave formed by cattails. Notice the means by which many of the details that are mentioned have been located.

33   Edwin Way Teale in "Adventure in Viewpoint"

From outside my little cave in the swamp tangle came sounds, each bringing its mental picture. The creaking clatter of the long-billed marsh wren, for all the world like the noise of a miniature unoiled lawn mower, presented to the mind's eye the vision 5 of its little body rising on vibrating wings a dozen feet into the air and then dropping back again in the manner of one of those tin helicopters we used to send aloft as boys. There were other noises: the far-carrying clang of metal, the yelp of a dog, the faint 10 drone of a high-flying plane, the cry of a gull coasting across the patch of sky above my cavern.

The air around me was filled with the faint sweetish perfume of the boneset * blooms. In a cluster hardly more than an inch in diameter, I counted ¹⁵ forty flowerets. Close beside me a wild bee alighted and, grasping a small clump of blooms with its forelegs as though holding a goblet, ran its long tongue into floweret after floweret. Brilliant little gold-banded flies walked up and down the green high- ²⁰ ways of the cattail leaves. On one dying leaf — brown along the edges, rich green beside the central rib, and yellow between — a fly with pinkish eyes, gold-white stripes down its face, and a tail tipped with red, basked in the sun. Below, on the ²⁵ floor of the cavern where an old cattail lay like a burst bomb, a gray fly with reddish eyes washed its face, kittenwise, over and over again.

* **boneset:** a type of flowering herb.

The Writer's Craft

1. Where is the reader informed about the vantage point from which the scene is being viewed? Why in a description is it effective for the writer to state his location where Teale does here?

2. Details in the first paragraph appeal to the sense of hearing. Are they coming from within the cave or outside it? How do you know? In line 12 what phrases locate the gull's position?

3. The second paragraph describes objects within the cave. What words and phrases locate the following details?

the wild bee (line 16)
the gold-banded flies (lines 19–21)
the various colors on the dying cattail leaf (lines 21–23)
the fly with pinkish eyes (lines 23–25)
the gray fly with reddish eyes (lines 25–27)

4. Read the selection through, omitting phrases that locate the details. Without those phrases does the selection create a vivid impression in your imagination? Explain why it was necessary to locate details in this description.

1. Comparisons using *like, as though,* and *as* add to the effectiveness of several of the details in this description. What similes make the following details vivid?

the clatter of the long-billed marsh wren (lines 3–5)
the way the bee grasps a small clump of blooms (lines 17–18)
the appearance of the old cattail on the floor of the cave (lines 26–27)

2. Having examined similes of other writers, try your hand at writing some of your own. What comparisons might give your reader a vivid impression of each of the following? Try to suggest several possibilities.

a. A baby learning to walk
b. The school yard a minute after the final bell rings before vacation
c. A miser counting his money
d. Someone waking up from a nightmare
e. Your feelings during a most embarrassing moment

Now You Try It

Describe a scene from a stationary vantage point, perhaps a street scene from a window, a landscape from the crest of a hill, a shoreline from a boat in the middle of a lake, a farm from a fence gate, or the skyline of a city from the top of a tall building. At the beginning of your composition, indicate the position from which you are viewing the scene. Locate the various details you mention, striving throughout to evoke a clear picture of the scene in your reader's imagination.

A MOVING VANTAGE POINT   A description of surroundings while the beholder is in motion — as, for example, when the view from a moving car is described — must necessarily be made from a moving vantage point. In imagining a scene depicted from such a vantage point, the writer would describe what is seen, heard, felt, and smelled in the progress forward. Details in such instances are located in relation to the position of the observer and to the surrounding scene. The following selection, describing a passage over the Red River between Oklahoma and Texas in the last century, is an example of a description written from a moving vantage point.

34   William Humphrey in *The Ordways*

Resigned at last to crossing over, the oxen pushed out towards midstream. They swam scared, but powerfully, straining into the yoke, which rode far down their necks. Then, about a hundred yards out, they struck the current. Those in the wagon felt it. 5 It came with no sudden jolt; to look at, the river here was hardly faster than inshore. But against the side of the wagon it bore down with tremendous pressure, like a bed of lava in its slow inexorable advance. They had their ballast of tombstones to 10 thank that they were not tipped over. It was as if the water were rapidly congealing, and the oxen, rearing themselves in leaps, their humps breaking water like fishes' fins, appeared to be struggling to extricate themselves from some thick and sticky 15 fluid. They began to lose headway and were borne irresistibly downstream. The landing, the road between the trees on the Texas shore, slipped behind. Yet the wagon still did not pitch, scarcely rocked, and although the waterline now lapped up to within 20 a scant two inches of the top, inside all was dry.

Midway across, maybe a bit farther, the oxen faltered. They sank back. The yoke rode up their necks until it caught on their horns. When this happened the wagon was spun round, astern to the current. 25 Its broadside relieved of pressure, it rose, and with it, floundering helplessly, rose the oxen. They shot downstream. Throughout all this, and all that followed, hardly a sound broke the stillness. Like molasses, the smooth brown river flowed heavily on its 30 way, indifferent to its passengers, and along both wooded shores a drowsy stillness reigned.

The oxen tried to break out of the current. When they veered aside (and the Ordways were willing now to let them choose their bank) the strain bowed [35] the wagon tongue. Then could be seen how powerful the silent and scarcely visible current was: breaking over the bent and quivering wagon tongue the water rippled like shot silk, drawn taut. For an instant then the wagon would hang broadside in the [40] current, shaking, while the team churned up and down, getting no place; then they would fade, sink back, spent, wheezing for breath, tongues lolling, drift helplessly around, and again be sped downstream. [45]

The Writer's Craft

1. Throughout the selection what words let you know the direction in which the wagon is moving in relation to the river? In what order are details presented? Is the order, for example, a random one, or are details arranged in ascending order of importance, or are they presented in some other way? Explain why the order in which they are presented is appropriate.

2. Throughout the selection the narrator locates details, as well as the position of the wagon in relation to its surroundings. What phrases locate the following details?

   a. The current when first encountered (lines 4–5)
   b. The landing and the road between the trees on the Texas shore (lines 17–18)
   c. The point where the yoke catches on the horns of the oxen (lines 23–24)
   d. The point where the wagon is spun around, astern to the current (lines 24–25)
   e. The point at which the strength of the current can be seen (lines 36–39)
   f. The point where the team of oxen sink back, wheezing for breath (lines 39–43)

3. How would you characterize the overall impression of this passage — as serene, tempestuous, routine, frightening, or what? What details in the selection most effectively support that impression?

Now You Try It

Write a description from a moving vantage point — perhaps a recollection of what you have seen while walking or bicycling somewhere, while traveling in a car, a boat, a plane, or a bus, or while riding on a ski lift or ferris wheel. Begin by establishing your general location and the fact that you were moving. Present appropriate sensory details in the order in which you encountered them. Probably you will want to limit the territory you describe so that your composition consists of approximately 200 words.

Sentence Skills

The effectiveness of a composition depends to a great extent on the writer's choice of words and the skill with which he arranges them in sentences. The following pages examine sentence-building skills used by writers of the models in the Description Section. Exercises covering sentence skills for other sections occur on the following pages: Narration (pages 105–12), Exposition (pages 143–47), Opinion and Persuasion (pages 176–79), Special Forms (pages 212–16).

POSITION OF ADJECTIVES

29 **Thomas Wolfe**
   in *Of Time and the River* (page 47)

Consider the position of the italicized adjectives in the following list of extracts from Wolfe's description of October. Then answer the questions below the list.

the granaries are *full*   *great red* barns
rich brown oozings   *clean dry* crunching
the fly gets *old* and *fat* and *blue*   oak leaves, *big* and *brown*
hard yellow rows   *sharp acrid* smoke

1. Do most adjectives come before or after the words they modify?
2. In which of the extracts do you find predicate adjectives — adjectives that follow a linking verb? What part of a sentence do predicate adjectives modify?
3. "Oak leaves, *big* and *brown*" could have been written "*big brown* oak leaves." In which word order are the oak leaves themselves emphasized more? Can you think of a reason why the author used "oak leaves, big and brown"?

As you have seen, adjectives may be placed in any of three positions: (1) before the word they modify, as in "*rich brown* oozings" (the usual position); (2) after a linking verb, as in "the granaries are *full*"; (3) directly after the word they modify, as in "oak leaves, *big* and *brown*." You have also seen that adjectives may be used singly or in two's or three's: "the granaries are *full*"; "*great red* barns"; "the fly gets *old* and *fat* and *blue*."

■ **EXERCISE A** Rewrite each of the following sentences, moving the italicized adjectives into as many different positions as you can. Your new sentences may not be better than the originals, but by writing them you will learn how the position of adjectives may be varied.

Example: This *rich* and *lazy* man leads a life of ease.
Rewritten: This man is *rich* and *lazy* and leads a life of ease.
　　　　　This man, *rich* and *lazy*, leads a life of ease.

After writing the sentences, notice the different effects you have created. Consider, for example, whether moving the adjectives changes the emphasis or alters the rhythm.

1. A *tall, muscular* bystander finally broke up the fight.
2. *Witty* and *good-natured*, she keeps her class in stitches.
3. The room is *spacious* and *light* and makes an ideal library.
4. A cloud, *dark* and *heavy*, was moving across the bay toward us.
5. Like a *great white* bird, the plane swung in an ascending arc away from the airport toward the hills, *low* and *dark* on the horizon.

■ **EXERCISE B** Add adjectives to each of the following sentences. In sentences 1 and 4 merely supply words for the blanks. In the others put in adjectives to modify the italicized words. Use some adjectives alone and some in pairs; place some before and some after the word modified; include some predicate adjectives. After you have finished, compare your sentences with those of your classmates. You may be surprised at the variety of adjectives and the ways they have been used.

1. A man who came to the door of the house said that he was _____ and _____ from his journey.
2. The *bicycle* lay in a *heap* on the *lawn*.
3. *Hedges* bordered the *path*.
4. The sun sank slowly behind the hills, leaving the sky_____ and _____.
5. The *sides* of the *stadium* towered above the *field*.

34 William Humphrey in *The Ordways* (page 61)

One way to add interest to writing is by varying the lengths of your sentences. The paragraph below, from William Humphrey's *The Ordways*, is a good example of pleasing variety in sentence lengths.

Midway across, maybe a bit farther, the oxen faltered. They sank back. The yoke rode up their necks until it caught on their horns. When this happened the wagon was spun round, astern to the current. Its broadside relieved of pressure, it rose, and with it, floundering helplessly, rose the oxen. They shot downstream. Throughout all this, and all that followed, hardly a sound broke the stillness. Like molasses, the smooth brown river flowed heavily on its way, indifferent to its passengers, and along both wooded shores a drowsy stillness reigned.

The number of words in each sentence in Humphrey's paragraph is as follows: first sentence: 9 words; second sentence: 3 words; third sentence: 12 words; fourth sentence: 12 words; fifth sentence: 15 words; sixth sentence: 3 words; seventh sentence: 13 words; eighth sentence: 24 words. If the author had split his long sentences into shorter ones, so that they all had approximately the same number of words, the result might have read something like this:

Midway across, the oxen began to falter. They sank back, as their yokes moved forward. When this happened the wagon was spun around. It floated astern to the swirling current. The broadside relieved of pressure, it rose. With it, floundering helplessly, rose the oxen. Almost at once the beasts shot downstream. Throughout all this, hardly a sound was heard. The brown smooth river flowed on its way. Along both shores a drowsy stillness reigned.

What effect is produced by this paragraph with sentences of approximately equal length? Why is the original paragraph more effective?

■ **EXERCISE**   Rewrite the following paragraph so that it contains sentences of varying lengths.

He was an old man. His back was bent. His bushy hair was white. His hands were gnarled. Under his arm he carried a silver knife. He also carried a lumpy cloth bundle. He also had a book. Its pages were ragged. They were yellow, too. Slowly he sat down under a tree. He opened the book. He began to read. His lips were moving. We could hear a low murmur. We edged closer. He couldn't see or hear us. But we could hear him a little better now. The words he read were old. They were also familiar. We came out from our hiding place. We sat down near him. We listened. He continued reading without so much as a glance at us.

Narration

LESSON **10**

Skills of Narration

Narratives tell stories. Events depicted in narrative writing may actually have happened or they may be wholly or partly a product of the writer's imagination, but whether a story is fact or fiction or a combination of both, telling it effectively calls for the use of specific techniques. Wolcott Gibbs has employed many of those techniques in writing the following narrative, which depicts an experience he had when he was a boy.

35   Wolcott Gibbs in "Do Re Mi"

I must have been ten when it came to me that never, this side of paradise, would I be able to carry a tune, and even identifying one would tax my tiny powers unless I could hear the words. I was a pupil then at the Horace Mann School, up on   5
120th Street, and our class was an early venture in experimental education, being held outdoors, on a roof. We wore little woolly suits and hoods that gave a sort of startled and bloodthirsty pleasure to the regular students downstairs, who were without   10
our embarrassing advantages. We looked like rabbits and when we ventured recklessly down from our roof during recess we were hunted like rabbits. We were like rabbits, too, in that we were the soft and foolish victims of a thousand grim experiments.   15

It was a thin week that didn't bring us at least one
delegation of educators of a refined and scientific
aspect, who came with their questionnaires and
went away to write admiringly about us in the jour-
nals of their trade. I never had to read these arti- 20
cles, but nevertheless I was grateful when one of
the bloodless creatures slipped on the icy roof and
broke his glasses.

The delegation which found out that I was tone-
deaf consisted of two ladies, who wished to test the 25
preadolescent reaction to music. We were lined up
in a solemn, woolly row while one of them wrote a
line of strange words on the blackboard. Her hand-
writing was distinguished, requiring quite a lot of
preliminary skirmishing with the chalk, and I had 30
begun to itch by the time the other one got up and
sang the words.

"Do re mi fa sol la ti do," she sang.

Our visitor sang the line two or three times more,
and then two or three times backward. 35

"Now, children," she said. "Let's all sing."

We all sang. At first we were uncertain, puzzled
by the unfamiliar words.

"Do I hear some little mice squeaking?" said the
first lady, cupping her hand gaily at her ear. "Oh, 40
come, children, let's have some really truly singing. Now louder . . ."

We sang louder, and presently, getting into the
spirit of the thing, we were yelling our heads off.
The ladies must have been new at preadolescent 45
research, because, having asked for really truly
singing, they seemed a little agitated when they
got it.

"That's fine," the first one said hastily. "Now we'll
let each child see what he can do all by his lone- 50
some. We'll start down at this end. What's your
name, little man?"

"Thomas," said Thomas, "but I don't sing."

"Why, Thomas!" said the second lady. "You don't
want to hurt Miss Edgerton's feelings, do you? 55
Now, 'Do' . . ."

"No," said Thomas firmly, but the ladies were too tough for him, and in the end he executed an embarrassed scale.

They moved down the line with varying results. Some of the children sang loud and clear, without self-consciousness, and were disappointed when the ladies moved on. Others were shy, and their singing was unhappy and almost inaudible. The ladies carefully noted these facts in their little notebooks.

I was not at all nervous when they came to me. They had said they wanted volume, and I was confident that I could sing as loud as anybody.

"And what is our name?" asked the first lady, who couldn't possibly have had any idea what she was in for.

I told her and then, as she tossed her head musically, I sang a hearty scale. Both ladies looked incredulous.

"Perhaps we'd better try again," said the second one, after a moment.

It seemed clear that I had been a disappointment to her, although I couldn't see why, because I was sure I had sung as loud as anybody else. I drew a deep breath and tried again. The ladies looked at one another.

"No," said the first, "I'm afraid we don't quite understand. The little notes go up like this."

She sang me a sample scale, with gestures that went up.

"Try to think of eight little men climbing a flight of stairs. Now . . ."

I sang again. The eight little men seemed to have no especial bearing on what I was doing, but I thought of them.

"It's amazing," said the second lady, though clearly this was not praise. "The child just stays on the same note."

"Completely tone-deaf," said the other one, and wrote briskly in her book.

They were reluctant to give me up, and produced many ingenious and graphic illustrations of the fact that the diatonic scale goes up as it goes along. I did my best, too, getting quite damp and breathless, to sing the way they wanted me to. My wool 100 pants were itching at the end, but I was still singing the same note, and the ladies were licked.

Later in life being tone-deaf had its advantages, but at Horace Mann it gave me a peculiar and grisly distinction. The children were not exactly 105 sure what was the matter with me, but whatever it was it had been sinister enough to alarm the investigators, and my playmates were impressed. For the rest of the year my singing had a fascination for them second only to the manual-training teach- 110 er's thumb, which had been bitten off by a turtle he'd been annoying.

The Writer's Craft

SELECTION OF EVENTS

The experience on which a narrative is based comprises a great many events. But a writer will select only those events that help him achieve the effect he seeks in telling the story. If, for example, he seeks to entertain the reader by telling a funny story, he will include only those aspects of the experience that contribute to the humor. If he wants to reveal character, he will select events that most effectively provide insights into the people being portrayed.

In this narrative Wolcott Gibbs seems intent in part on amusing the reader with a humorous account of the day he discovered his tonedeafness. Accordingly, from the many events that occurred in the course of that day, he has selected only those that help create an amusing story about that discovery. The narrative consists of four main events. The first concerns the visiting delegation's presentation of the scale to the children (lines 24–36); the second, the class's singing the scale as a group (lines 37–48). The third event takes place in lines 49–59. What happens in those lines? In lines 60–65, why do you suppose the author summarizes the individual efforts of most of the class, instead of presenting each child's attempt in detail? The final event is depicted in lines 66–102. What is it? Why is it presented in great detail?

The *introduction* of a narrative should identify the situation and supply any necessary background information while arousing the reader's interest. Where in the first paragraph does the author name the experience he is going to write about? Why do you suppose he includes in that paragraph details about the everyday activities of his classmates at the Horace Mann School? How does he arouse interest in the narrative at the start?

The *development* of a narrative relates the main events of the story, usually in chronological order. Consider the events in "Do Re Mi." Are they presented chronologically, or does the author skip backward and forward in time? Why is it usually effective to organize a narrative chronologically?

The *conclusion* should bring the narrative to a satisfying end; that is, the reader should feel that the author has given a complete account of the story he set out to tell. How is "Do Re Mi" concluded? Explain why the conclusion is or is not satisfactory for this narrative.

USE OF NARRATIVE DETAILS

Examine the following list, which reveals the purposes of some of the details in Gibbs's narrative.

Details that make actions specific:

> Her handwriting was distinguished, requiring quite a lot of preliminary skirmishing with the chalk . . . (lines 28–30)
>
> We sang louder, and presently, getting into the spirit of the thing, we were yelling our heads off. (lines 43–44)
>
> The ladies carefully noted these facts in their little note-books. (lines 64–65)

Details that explain:

> . . . our class was an early venture in experimental education, being held outdoors, on a roof. (lines 6–8)
>
> The delegation which found out that I was tone-deaf consisted of two ladies, who wished to test the preadolescent reaction to music. (lines 24–26)
>
> Later in life being tone-deaf had its advantages, but at Horace Mann it gave me a peculiar and grisly distinction. (lines 103–05)

Skills of Narration **75**

Details that help the reader visualize the scene:

> We wore little woolly suits and hoods . . . (line 8)

> We looked like rabbits . . . (lines 11–12)

> We were lined up in a solemn, woolly row while one of them wrote a line of strange words on the blackboard. (lines 26–28)

Details that reveal character:

> The ladies must have been new at preadolescent research, because, having asked for really truly singing, they seemed a little agitated when they got it. (lines 45–48)

> I was not at all nervous when they came to me. (line 66)

> They were reluctant to give me up, and produced many ingenious and graphic illustrations of the fact that the diatonic scale goes up as it goes along. (lines 96–98)

> I did my best, too, getting quite damp and breathless, to sing the way they wanted me to. (lines 99–100)

USE OF DIALOGUE

Dialogue is quoted conversation of characters in a narrative or drama. On three occasions in "Do Re Mi" the story is told primarily by means of dialogue (lines 36–42; lines 49–59; lines 69–95). Reread those lines and explain why they are effective. Does the dialogue sound natural? Does it help create a feeling that the events are actually happening?

In addition to conveying information and moving the action forward, dialogue helps reveal personality. What, for example, do the following lines tell you about the women visitors and about Thomas?

> "That's fine," the first one said hastily. "Now we'll let each child see what he can do all by his lonesome. We'll start down at this end. What's your name, little man?"
>
> "Thomas," said Thomas, "but I don't sing."
>
> "Why, Thomas!" said the second lady. "You don't want to hurt Miss Edgerton's feelings, do you? Now, 'Do' . . ."
>
> "No," said Thomas firmly, but the ladies were too tough for him, and in the end he executed an embarrassed scale.

POINT OF VIEW

In writing a narrative, the author must decide from what point of view he will tell it — whether from within the action, as a participant, or from a point totally outside it. "Do Re Mi" is told from a participant's point of view; the author speaks as the "I" in the story.

In telling a story from the point of view of a participant, a writer is limited to his own observations and feelings. He may depict what he and the other people involved did; he may interpret the reactions of others; but he cannot reveal the unspoken thoughts and feelings of anyone other than himself. Find at least three places in "Do Re Mi" where the author reveals his own feelings and thoughts during the experience.

Now You Try It

"Do Re Mi" is based on an amusing boyhood experience. Following that lead, think back on your own past or recent experiences and choose one that seems especially humorous. In a narrative several paragraphs long, of approximately 350–400 words, relate that experience, including only what is most significant and humorous about it. Use narrative details and dialogue, and tell the story from the point of view of a participant in the action.

LESSON **11**

Selecting Events

Several criteria guide the selection of events to be included in a narrative. In general, only those events should be chosen that (1) help move the action forward, (2) reveal the character of people involved in the action, and (3) add interest to the story, perhaps by making it suspenseful, humorous, or moving. A single event may serve one or more of these purposes.

In the following narrative notice the events Lincoln Steffens has included to evoke a Christmas recalled from his childhood.

36   Lincoln Steffens in
   The Autobiography of Lincoln Steffens

What interested me in our new neighborhood was not the school, nor the room I was to have in the house all to myself, but the stable which was built back of the house. My father let me direct the making of a stall, a little smaller than the other 5
stalls, for my pony, and I prayed and hoped and my sister Lou believed that I would get the pony, perhaps for Christmas. I pointed out to her that there were three other stalls and no horses at all. This I said in order that she should answer it. She 10
could not. My father, sounded,* said that some day we might have horses and a cow; meanwhile a

* **sounded:** questioned.

stable added to the value of a house. "Someday" is a pain to a boy who lives in and knows only "now." My good little sisters, to comfort me, re- 15 marked that Christmas was coming, but Christmas was always coming and grown-ups were always talking about it, asking you what you wanted and then giving you what they wanted you to have. Though everybody knew what I wanted, I told 20 them all again. My mother knew that I told God, too, every night. I wanted a pony, and to make sure that they understood, I declared that I wanted nothing else.

"Nothing but a pony?" my father asked. 25

"Nothing," I said.

"Not even a pair of high boots?"

That was hard. I did want boots, but I stuck to the pony. "No, not even boots."

"Not candy? There ought to be something to fill 30 your stocking with, and Santa Claus can't put a pony into a stocking."

That was true, and he couldn't lead a pony down the chimney either. But no. "All I want is a pony," I said. "If I can't have a pony, give me nothing, 35 nothing."

Now I had been looking myself for the pony I wanted, going to sales stables, inquiring of horse-men, and I had seen several that would do. My father let me "try" them. I tried so many ponies 40 that I was learning fast to sit a horse. I chose several, but my father always found some fault with them. I was in despair. When Christmas was at hand I had given up all hope of a pony, and on Christmas Eve I hung up my stocking along with 45 my sisters', of whom, by the way, I now had three. They were so happy that Christmas Eve that I caught some of their merriment. I speculated on what I'd get; I hung up the biggest stocking I had, and we all went reluctantly to bed to wait till 50 morning. Not to sleep; not right away. We were told that we must not only sleep promptly, we must not wake up till seven-thirty the next morn-

ing — or if we did, we must not go to the fireplace
for our Christmas. Impossible. ⁵⁵

We did sleep that night, but we woke up at six
A.M. We lay in our beds and debated through the
open doors whether to obey till, say, half-past six.
Then we bolted. I don't know who started it, but
there was a rush. We all disobeyed; we raced to ⁶⁰
disobey and get first to the fireplace in the front
room downstairs. And there they were, the gifts, all
sorts of wonderful things, mixed-up piles of presents; only, as I disentangled the mess, I saw that
my stocking was empty; it hung limp; not a thing ⁶⁵
in it; and under and around it — nothing. My sisters
had knelt down, each by her pile of gifts; they were
squealing with delight, till they looked up and saw
me standing there in my nightgown with nothing.
They left their piles to come to me and look with ⁷⁰
me at my empty place. Nothing. They felt my
stocking: nothing.

I don't know whether I cried at that moment, but
my sisters did. They ran with me back to my bed,
and there we all cried till I became indignant. That ⁷⁵
helped some. I got up, dressed, and driving my
sisters away, I went alone out into the yard, down
to the stable, and there, all by myself, I wept. My
mother came out to me by and by; she found me in
my pony stall, sobbing on the floor, and she tried to ⁸⁰
comfort me. But I heard my father outside; he had
come part way with her, and she was having some
sort of angry quarrel with him. She tried to comfort
me; besought me to come to breakfast. I could not;
I wanted no comfort and no breakfast. She left me ⁸⁵
and went into the house with sharp words for my
father.

I don't know what kind of breakfast the family
had. My sisters said it was "awful." They were
ashamed to enjoy their own toys. They came to me, ⁹⁰
and I was rude. I ran away from them. I went
around to the front of the house, sat down on the
steps, and, the crying over, I ached. I was wronged,
I was hurt — I can feel now what I felt then, and I

am sure that if one could see the wounds upon our 95
hearts, there would be found still upon mine a scar
from that terrible Christmas morning. And my father, the practical joker, he must have been hurt,
too, a little. I saw him looking out of the window.
He was watching me or something for an hour or 100
two, drawing back the curtain ever so little lest I
catch him, but I saw his face, and I think I can see
now the anxiety upon it, the worried impatience.

After — I don't know how long — surely an hour
or two — I was brought to the climax of my agony 105
by the sight of a man riding a pony down the street,
a pony and a brand-new saddle; the most beautiful
saddle I ever saw, and it was a boy's saddle; the
man's feet were not in the stirrups; his legs were
too long. The outfit was perfect; it was the realiza- 110
tion of all my dreams, the answer to my prayers. A
fine new bridle, with a light curb bit. And the pony!
As he drew near, I saw that the pony was really a
small horse, what we called an Indian pony, a bay,
with black mane and tail, and one white foot and 115
a white star on his forehead. For such a horse as
that I would have given, I could have forgiven,
anything.

But the man, a disheveled fellow with a blackened eye and a fresh-cut face, came along, reading 120
the numbers on the houses, and, as my hopes — my
impossible hopes — rose, he looked at our door and
passed by, he and the pony, and the saddle and the
bridle. Too much. I fell upon the steps, and having
wept before, I broke now into such a flood of tears 125
that I was a floating wreck when I heard a voice.

"Say, kid," it said, "do you know a boy named
Lennie Steffens?"

I looked up. It was the man on the pony, back
again, at our horse block. 130

"Yes," I spluttered through my tears. "That's me."

"Well," he said, "then this is your horse. I've been
looking all over for you and your house. Why don't
you put your number where it can be seen?"

"Get down," I said, running out to him. 135

He went on saying something about "ought to have got here at seven o'clock; told me to bring the nag here and tie him to your post and leave him for you. But, I got into a fight — and a hospital, and —"

"Get down," I said. 140

He got down, and he boosted me up to the saddle. He offered to fit the stirrups to me, but I didn't want him to. I wanted to ride.

"What's the matter with you?" he said, angrily. "What you crying for? Don't you like the horse? 145 He's a dandy, this horse. I know him of old. He's fine at cattle; he'll drive 'em along."

I hardly heard, I could scarcely wait, but he persisted. He adjusted the stirrups, and then, finally, off I rode, slowly, at a walk, so happy, so thrilled, 150 that I did not know what I was doing. I did not look back at the house or the man, I rode off up the street, taking note of everything — of the reins, of the pony's long mane, of the carved leather saddle. I had never seen anything so beautiful. And mine! 155 I was going to ride up past Miss Kay's house. But I noticed on the horn of the saddle some stains like raindrops, so I turned and trotted home, not to the house but to the stable. There was the family, father, mother, sisters, all working for me, all happy. 160 They had been putting in place the tools of my new business: blankets, currycomb, brush, pitchfork — everything, and there was hay in the loft.

"What did you come back so soon for?" somebody asked. "Why didn't you go on riding?" 165

I pointed to the stains. "I wasn't going to get my new saddle rained on," I said. And my father laughed. "It isn't raining," he said. "Those are not raindrops."

"They are tears," my mother gasped, and she 170 gave my father a look which sent him off to the house. Worse still, my mother offered to wipe away the tears still running out of my eyes. I gave her such a look as she had given him, and she went off after my father, drying her own tears. My sisters 175 remained and we all unsaddled the pony, put on his halter, led him to his stall, tied and fed him. It began really to rain; so all the rest of that memorable day we curried and combed that pony. The girls plaited his mane, forelock, and tail, while I pitch- [180] forked hay to him and curried and brushed, curried and brushed. For a change we brought him out to drink; we led him up and down, blanketed like a racehorse; we took turns at that. But the best, the most inexhaustible fun, was to clean him. When we [185] went reluctantly to our midday Christmas dinner, we all smelt of horse, and my sisters had to wash their faces and hands. I was asked to, but I wouldn't, till my mother bade me look in the mirror. Then I washed up — quick. My face was caked with the [190] muddy lines of tears that had coursed over my cheeks to my mouth. Having washed away that shame, I ate my dinner, and as I ate I grew hungrier and hungrier. It was my first meal that day, and as I filled up on the turkey and the stuffing, the cran- [195] berries and the pies, the fruits and the nuts — as I swelled, I could laugh. My mother said I still choked and sobbed now and then, but I laughed, too; I saw and enjoyed my sisters' presents till I had to go out and attend to my pony, who was there, [200] really and truly there, the promise, the beginning of a happy double life. And — I went and looked to make sure — there was the saddle, too, and the bridle.

But that Christmas, which my father had planned [205] so carefully, was it the best or the worst I ever knew? He often asked me that; I never could answer as a boy. I think now that it was both. It covered the whole distance from broken-hearted misery to bursting happiness — too fast. A grown-up [210] could hardly have stood it.

The Writer's Craft

1. This narrative tells of the time a boy longed for and finally received a pony for Christmas. Accordingly, events unrelated to that longing and its gratification are omitted. At the very begin-

ning we learn that the author that Christmas was living in a new neighborhood. Events related to his enrolling in a new school and making new friends must have been interesting. Why do you suppose nothing is said about them?

2. Steffens and his family must have had many discussions about the boy's desire for a pony. Yet the author includes only one such conversation in the narrative. Why were the others omitted?

3. Reconsider the events Steffens includes. What are some additional events that no doubt took place that Christmas day? Why were they omitted from the narrative?

4. In the first evening depicted in the narrative the stall was built (lines 1–13). This important event sets the scene and directs attention to the boy's desire to own a pony. The second event, discussing the Christmas presents (lines 15–36), develops the narrative by emphasizing the boy's wish for a pony. The other events in Steffens's narrative are listed below. Decide how each one contributes to the story. (Events may be included for one or more of the following reasons: to reveal character, to create suspense, to emphasize the purpose for which the story is being told, to move the action forward, to provide a turning point in the action, or to conclude the action.)

Steffens's inquiries about a pony for himself (lines 37–43)
Activities on Christmas Eve in the Steffens's home (lines 43–55)
Opening the stockings on Christmas morning (lines 56–72)
Steffens's retreat to the bedroom and then to the stable (lines 73–78)
Mr. and Mrs. Steffens going out to him in the stable (lines 78–87)
Breakfast time and Steffens sitting on the front steps (lines 88–103)
The arrival of the pony (lines 104–47)
The first ride on the pony (lines 148–75)
Caring for the pony in the stable (lines 175–85)
Christmas dinner (lines 185–99)
Steffens's enjoyment of his sisters' presents and his return to the stable (lines 199–204)

5. In a narrative the opening paragraph, or the first few paragraphs, should arouse the reader's interest while focusing the story by presenting necessary background information about characters and setting. What background information is given in the first paragraph of this selection? Is the paragraph necessary for an understanding of later events? Why, or why not?

6. Events take place in time. Accordingly, the writer of a narrative usually presents the events in chronological order, employing transitional expressions to indicate the passage of time or to show when something happened. Transitional expressions in this selection include *on Christmas Eve* (lines 44–45), *at six* A.M. (lines 56–57), *till half-past six* (line 58), and *at that moment* (line 73). Find at least three other transitional expressions used to indicate time sequence in the selection.

7. The events of a well-written narrative lead to an appropriate conclusion. How does Steffens conclude this narrative — with an event or with some general comments about that memorable Christmas? Do you find his conclusion effective? Why, or why not?

Now You Try It

Write a narrative of events that led to your obtaining something you badly wanted. Before beginning the narrative, list the events you plan to include, making sure that each contributes something to the development or interest of your story. Use the beginning paragraphs to give necessary background information, and bring the story to a satisfying conclusion. Events should be presented in chronological order, with transitional expressions clarifying the time when each event occurred.

LESSON **12**
Using Narrative Details

The writer of an effective narrative presents details in a way that makes events both colorful and interesting. Unless he does so, his narrative will be simply a series of flat statements, as unemphatic as a routine log book or an accident report.

The following selection describes the conquest of Everest, the highest mountain in the world. As you read Sir Edmund Hillary's account of his and Tenzing Norgay's assault on the peak, try to determine why the events being described stand out vividly in your mind.

37   Sir Edmund Hillary in "The Summit"

The weather for Everest seemed practically perfect. Insulated as we were in all our down clothing and windproofs, we suffered no discomfort from cold or wind. However, on one occasion I removed my sunglasses to examine more closely a difficult ⁵ section of the ridge but was very soon blinded by the fine snow driven by the bitter wind and hastily replaced them. I went on cutting steps. To my surprise I was enjoying the climb as much as I had ever enjoyed a fine ridge in my own New Zealand ¹⁰ Alps.

After an hour's steady going we reached the foot of the most formidable looking problem on the ridge — a rock step some forty feet high. We had known of the existence of this step from aerial pho- [15] tographs and had also seen it through our binoculars from Thyangboche. We realized that at this altitude it might well spell the difference between success and failure. The rock itself, smooth and almost holdless, might have been an interesting afternoon [20] problem to a group of expert rock climbers in the Lake District, but here it was a barrier beyond our feeble strength to overcome. I could see no way of turning it on the steep rock bluff on the west, but fortunately another possibility of tackling it still re- [25] mained. On its east side was another great cornice * and running up the full forty feet of the step was a narrow crack between the cornice and the rock. Leaving Tenzing to belay ° me as best he could, I jammed my way into this crack, then kicking back- [30] ward with my crampons † I sank their spikes deep into the frozen snow behind me and levered myself off the ground. Taking advantage of every little rock hold and all the force of knee, shoulder, and arms I could muster, I literally cramponed backward up [35] the crack, with a fervent prayer that the cornice would remain attached to the rock. Despite the considerable effort involved, my progress although slow was steady, and as Tenzing paid out the rope I inched my way upward until I could finally reach [40] over the top of the rock and drag myself out of the crack onto a wide ledge. For a few moments I lay regaining my breath and for the first time really felt the fierce determination that nothing now could stop our reaching the top. I took a firm stance on the [45] ledge and signaled to Tenzing to come on up. As I heaved hard on the rope Tenzing wriggled his way up the crack and finally collapsed exhausted at the top like a giant fish when it has been hauled from the sea after a terrible struggle. [50]

---

* **cornice:** a mass of drifted snow clinging to and overhanging the crest of a ridge.
° **belay:** hold fast by pulling a rope around a pin.
† **crampons:** climbing irons.

I checked both our oxygen sets and roughly calculated our flow rates. Everything seemed to be going well. Probably owing to the strain imposed on him by the trouble with his oxygen set, Tenzing had been moving rather slowly but he was climbing [55] safely, and this was the major consideration. His only comment on my inquiring of his condition was to smile and wave along the ridge. We were going to cut down our flow rate to two liters per minute if the extra endurance was required. [60]

The ridge continued as before. Giant cornices on the right, steep rock slopes on the left. I went on cutting steps on the narrow strip of snow. The ridge curved away to the right and we had no idea where the top was. As I cut around the back of one hump, [65] another higher one would swing into view. Time was passing and the ridge seemed never-ending. In one place where the angle of the ridge had eased off, I tried cramponing without cutting steps, hoping this would save time, but I quickly realized that [70] our margin of safety on these steep slopes at this altitude was too small, so I went on step cutting. I was beginning to tire a little now. I had been cutting steps continuously for two hours, and Tenzing, too, was moving very slowly. As I chipped steps around [75] still another corner, I wondered rather dully just how long we could keep it up. Our original zest had now quite gone and it was turning into a grim struggle. I then realized that the ridge ahead, instead of still monotonously rising, now dropped sharply [80] away, and far below I could see the North Col and the Rongbuk Glacier. I looked upward to see a narrow snow ridge running up to a snowy summit. A few more whacks of the ice ax in the firm snow and we stood on top. [85]

My initial feelings were of relief — relief that there were no more steps to cut — no more ridges to traverse and no more humps to tantalize us with hopes of success. I looked at Tenzing and in spite of the balaclava,* goggles, and oxygen mask all encrusted [90]

* **balaclava:** a knitted cap worn by mountaineers.

with long icicles that concealed his face, there was
no disguising his infectious grin of pure delight as
he looked all around him. We shook hands and then
Tenzing threw his arms around my shoulders and
we thumped each other on the back until we were ⁹⁵
almost breathless.

The Writer's Craft

1. Instead of merely recording a matter-of-fact account of his
successful assault on Everest, Hillary uses skills of narrative
writing in presenting details that help the reader appreciate the
difficulties and excitement of the venture. Some of the narrative
details included enable the reader to see what is happening. How
do the following details help you visualize the climbers, their
actions, and the setting?

> Insulated as we were in all our down clothing and wind-
> proofs, we suffered no discomfort from cold or wind. (lines
> 2–4)

> . . . I jammed my way into this crack, then kicking back-
> ward with my crampons I sank their spikes deep into the
> frozen snow behind me and levered myself off the ground.
> (lines 29–33)

> . . . Tenzing wriggled his way up the crack and finally col-
> lapsed exhausted at the top like a giant fish when it has
> been hauled from the sea after a terrible struggle. (lines
> 47–50)

> The ridge continued as before. Giant cornices on the right,
> steep rock slopes on the left. (lines 61–62)

Find at least three other narrative details that help you see the
climbers, their actions, or the setting. Cite specific lines from the
selection.

2. Details may reveal the feelings of people involved in the
action. The author reports that, having climbed to the top of the
rock, he lay regaining his breath for a few minutes "and for the
first time really *felt the fierce determination that nothing now
could stop our reaching the top.*" At the end of the selection he
describes his feelings on reaching the summit. How does he say
he felt? How did Tenzing feel? Why is it effective to describe
people's feelings in a narrative? In answering, remember that

forceful narrative writing seeks to recapture experience and make it seem real.

3. Details may furnish reasons and explanations for actions. Details in this selection explain why the rock step presented such a formidable obstacle: it was forty feet high; it was too smooth to provide a handhold or toehold; and there seemed to be no way around it. Instead of explaining why the rock posed a serious problem, suppose the author had simply said: "We came to a rock step, which presented a formidable obstacle to our progress." Compare that statement with lines 12–28 of the selection. On the basis of the comparison, what would seem to be some of the advantages of including details that offer explanations?

WORD CHOICE: VIVID VERBS AND VERB FORMS

The selection evokes a clear and dramatic picture, partly through the use of verbs and verb forms (participles, gerunds, and infinitives) that describe specific actions. Consider the sentence in lines 29–33: "Leaving Tenzing to belay me as best he could, I jammed my way into this crack, then kicking backward with my crampons I sank their spikes deep into the frozen snow behind me and levered myself off the ground." Instead of the infinitive *to hold,* the author uses *to belay,* which describes a specific manner of holding. He writes, "I *jammed* my way . . ." thus evoking a vivid image of the way he forced his body into the crack. Similarly, "*levered* myself off the ground" gives a clear picture of how he raised his body. Now look back at the selection and find as many other vivid verbs and verb forms as you can.

Now You Try It

Turn one of the following summaries into a story by adding narrative details that will enable the reader to see the setting, characters, and action. Be sure to include details to explain why the various events occur and to reveal how the various characters feel.

> a. This was the most important game of the season. During most of it I remained on the bench, but in the fourth quarter the coach was short of players, so he let me go in. In the final seconds of the game, I caught a pass and ran for a touchdown. The fans went wild.

b. I was a little younger then. The so-called friends dared me to meet them at midnight in the cemetery at the edge of town, in order to initiate me into a newly formed club of adventurers. I sneaked out, and down through a tough section of the city, finally reaching the cemetery just as it started to rain. Nobody was there. Midnight. Nothing happened for a while, and then suddenly I saw something white and spooky moving slowly toward me from the direction of a huge tombstone. I screamed and ran, hearing very unghostly laughter behind me as I fled.

c. Mary came over to spend the weekend with her friend Susan. All went well until Sunday morning, at church, when Mary found herself trying to stifle a recurrence of the giggling fit in which the girls had been caught up the night before. It really wasn't funny; Susan noted it with horror. The minister was at prayer, and all the congregation was solemn and hushed, and yet before long Susan was having to fight back giggles, too. Finally, to the annoyance of her parents, she had to tiptoe out as though she were going for a drink of water to ease the cough she had pretended was bothering her. Mary joined her outside a minute or two later.

d. My friends and I wanted to experiment, so we bought a home-permanent kit at the drugstore. Linda was our first victim. We began by cutting her hair. But not being professional we didn't get the hairline even. We tried to fix it, but the hair kept getting shorter. Next we followed the directions and put on the wave lotion. Halfway through the process, the phone rang. It was for Linda. She talked for twenty minutes. In the meantime the lotion was doing its job. When we rinsed her hair, we found it was tightly curled. Linda was angry, but there was little we could do. Finally we decided to help her pay for a trip to the beauty parlor.

LESSON **13**

Using Dialogue

Dialogue in a story helps bring events to life. By quoting what people say exactly, the writer adds interest and a sense of immediacy to the events he is recording. Notice what the dialogue adds to the following narrative.

38 Frank B. Gilbreth, Jr. and Ernestine Gilbreth Carey in *Cheaper by the Dozen*

At about the time that he brought home the victrolas, Dad became a consultant to the Remington typewriter company and, through motion study methods, helped Remington develop the world's fastest typist.   5

He told us about it one night at dinner — how he had put little flashing lights on the fingers of the typist and taken moving pictures and time exposures to see just what motions she employed and how those motions could be reduced.   10

"Anyone can learn to type fast," Dad concluded. "Why, I've got a system that will teach touch typing in two weeks. Absolutely guaranteed."

You could see the Great Experiment hatching in his mind.   15

"In two weeks," he repeated. "Why I could even

teach a child to type touch system in two weeks."

"Can you type touch system, Daddy?" Bill asked.

"In two weeks," said Dad. "I could teach a child. Anybody can do it if he will do just exactly what I tell him to do."

The next day he brought home a new, perfectly white typewriter, a gold knife, and an Ingersoll watch. He unwrapped them and put them on the dining room table.

"Can I try the typewriter, Daddy?" asked Mart.

"Why is the typewriter white?" Anne wanted to know. "All typewriters I've ever seen were black. It's beautiful, all right, but why is it white?"

"It's white so that it will photograph better," Dad explained. "Also, for some reason, anyone who sees a white typewriter wants to type on it. Don't ask me why. It's psychology."

All of us wanted to use it, but Dad wouldn't let anyone touch it but himself.

"This is an optional experiment," he said. "I believe I can teach the touch system in two weeks. Anyone who wants to learn will be able to practice on the white machine. The one who can type the fastest at the end of two weeks will receive the typewriter as a present. The knife and watch will be prizes awarded on a handicap basis, taking age into consideration."

Except for the two youngest, who still weren't talking, we all said we wanted to learn.

"Can I practice first, Daddy?" Bill asked.

"No one practices until I say 'practice.' Now first I will show you how the typewriter works." Dad got a sheet of paper. "The paper goes in here. You turn this — so-oo. And you push the carriage over to the end of the line — like this."

And Dad, using two fingers, hesitatingly pecked out the first thing that came to his mind — his name.

"Is that the touch system, Daddy?" Bill asked.

"No," said Dad. "I'll show you the touch system in a little while."

"Do you know the touch system, Daddy?"

"Let's say I know how to teach it, Billy boy."

"But do you know it yourself, Daddy?"

"I know how to teach it," Dad shouted. "In two weeks I can teach it to a child. Do you hear me? I have just finished helping to develop the fastest typist in the world. Do you hear that? They tell me Caruso's voice teacher can't sing a by-jingoed note. Does that answer your question?"

"I guess so," said Bill.

"Any other questions?"

There weren't. Dad then brought out some paper diagrams of a typewriter keyboard, and passed one to each of us.

"The first thing you have to do is to memorize the keyboard. QWERTYUIOP. Those are the letters in the top line. Memorize them. Get to know them forward and backwards. Get to know them so you can say them with your eyes closed. Like this."

Dad closed his right eye, but kept his left open just a slit so that he could still read the chart.

"QWERTYUIOP. See what I mean? Get to know them in your sleep. That's the first step."

We looked crestfallen.

"I know. You want to try out that white typewriter. Pretty, isn't it?"

He clicked a few keys.

"Runs as smoothly as a watch, doesn't it?"

We said it did.

"Well, tomorrow or the next day you'll be using it. First you have to memorize the keyboard. Then you've got to learn what fingers to use. Then you'll graduate to Moby Dick here. And one of you will win him."

Once we had memorized the keyboard, our fingers were colored with chalk. The little fingers were colored blue, the index fingers red, and so forth. Corresponding colors were placed on the key zones of the diagrams. For instance, the Q, A, and Z, all of which are hit with the little finger of the left hand, were colored blue to match the blue little finger.

"All you have to do now is practice until each finger has learned the right color habit," Dad said. [100] "And once you've got that, we'll be ready to start."

In two days we were fairly adept at matching the colors on our fingers with the colors on the keyboard diagrams. Ernestine was the fastest, and got the first chance to sit down at the white typewriter. [105] She hitched her chair up to it confidently, while we all gathered around.

"Hey, no fair, Daddy," she wailed. "You've put blank caps on all the keys. I can't see what I'm typing." [110]

Blank caps are fairly common now, but Dad had thought up the idea and had had them made specially by the Remington company.

"You don't have to see," Dad said. "Just imagine that those keys are colored, and type just like you [115] were typing on the diagram."

Ern started slowly, and then picked up speed, as her fingers jumped instinctively from key to key. Dad stood in back of her, with a pencil in one hand and a diagram in the other. Every time she made a [120] mistake, he brought the pencil down on the top of her head.

"Stop it, Daddy. That hurts. I can't concentrate knowing that the pencil's about to descend on my head." [125]

"It's meant to hurt. Your head has to teach your fingers not to make mistakes."

Ern typed along. About every fifth word, she'd make a mistake and the pencil would descend with a bong. But the bongs became less and less fre- [130] quent and finally Dad put away the pencil.

"That's fine, Ernie," he said. "I believe I'll keep you."

By the end of the two weeks, all children over six years old and Mother knew the touch system [135] reasonably well. Dad said he knew it too. We were a long way from being fast — because nothing but practice gives speed — but we were reasonably accurate.

Dad entered Ernestine's name in a national speed 140
contest, as a sort of child prodigy, but Mother
talked him out of it and Ern never actually com-
peted.

"It's not that I want to show her off," he told
Mother. "It's just that I want to do the people a fa- 145
vor — to show them what can be done with proper
instruction methods and motion study."

"I don't think it would be too good an idea,
dear," Mother said. "Ernestine is high strung, and
the children are conceited enough as it is." 150

Dad compromised by taking moving pictures of
each of us, first with colored fingers practicing on
the paper diagrams and then actually working on
the typewriter. He said the pictures were "for my
files," but about a month later they were released 155
in a newsreel, which showed everything except the
pencil descending on our heads. And some of us
today recoil every time we touch the backspace
key.

The Writer's Craft

1. Dialogue can show relationships between people and reveal their personalities. Reread lines 46–67 in the model. What
does dialogue in that passage tell you about Mr. Gilbreth? about
Bill? about the relationship between father and son?

Find other lines of dialogue in the narrative that indicate
something about Mr. Gilbreth as a teacher, as a psychologist, and
as a father. What does Mrs. Gilbreth's speech in lines 148–50 reveal about her personality?

2. Dialogue may also convey information about what is happening in a story. Notice how the following lines from the selection explain what Mr. Gilbreth intends to do in his experiment:

> "This is an optional experiment," he said. "I believe I can
> teach the touch system in two weeks. Anyone who wants to
> learn will be able to practice on the white machine. The
> one who can type the fastest at the end of two weeks will
> receive the typewriter as a present. The knife and watch
> will be prizes awarded on a handicap basis, taking age into
> consideration."

Find at least two other passages of dialogue that help explain what is happening in the story.

3. If dialogue is to be effective, it should sound natural. In other words, lines of dialogue attributed to a character should resemble the language that person would speak in the given situation. Naturally, the quoted lines should sound like spoken language, using the short sentences, sentence fragments, and contractions encountered in ordinary speech. Does the dialogue in this selection sound natural? In each case, is it appropriate to the character speaking? Support your answer by citing specific examples from the narrative.

4. By simply reporting what was said instead of making it seem that the various members of the family were actually speaking, the authors could have written this narrative without any dialogue at all. For example, here is one way that lines 11–17 might have been written without dialogue:

> Dad claimed that he had a system that would teach touch typing in two weeks and guaranteed that it would work.

After examining the dialogue in lines 11–17 and elsewhere in the model, explain what advantages the narrative gains from its inclusion.

DIALOGUE TAGS

To make clear who is speaking dialogue, an author starts a new paragraph each time a different person begins to speak, and when necessary he uses a *dialogue tag* to identify the speaker. Dialogue tags are italicized in the following lines from the model:

> "In two weeks," *he repeated*. "Why I could even teach a child to type touch system in two weeks."
> "Can you type touch system, Daddy?" *Bill asked*.

In addition to identifying the speaker, tags may indicate how the words were spoken:

> "I know how to teach it," Dad *shouted*.
> "Hey, no fair, Daddy," she *wailed*.

Often the context makes clear who is speaking and how; in such cases dialogue tags should be omitted. Lines 57–59 omit tags. Why are they unnecessary there? Are there any places in the narrative where the omission of tags leaves you confused about who is speaking, or how? If so, which speeches are they?

Now You Try It

Write a brief narrative either about a situation of your own choice or about one of the situations listed below. Use dialogue to convey information about what is happening, to show reactions, and to reveal personality. Try to write lines of dialogue that are appropriate to the speaker and to the situation. Start a new paragraph each time the speaker changes, and use tags wherever necessary either to indicate who is speaking or to tell in what tone of voice a speech is delivered. Be sure your narrative comes to a satisfying conclusion.

a. A father differs with his daughter about how much freedom girls of her age should have.
b. An older lady and a young girl discuss teen-age manners or lack of them.
c. A shy boy asks out a girl who isn't interested in him.
d. The quarterback is late to practice again, and the coach has had enough.
e. An interview for a summer job goes badly.
f. A student plans to drop out of school until a friend talks him out of it.

LESSON **14**

Point of View

To avoid confusion the events in a narrative should be observed from one point of view consistently. Sometimes the author will represent the narrator of the events as a participant in the action, observing firsthand what is going on. Such a story is said to be told from a *personal point of view*. At other times the writer as narrator stands outside the narrative, able to reveal the thoughts and actions of all the characters taking part in the events. Such a story is said to be written from an *omniscient*, or all-knowing, *point of view*. The models in this lesson demonstrate both narrative methods.

PERSONAL POINT OF VIEW   In *The Whispering Land* zoologist Gerald Durrell tells of an expedition he made to Argentina to collect animals for his private zoo in England. The following narrative, an excerpt from that book, describes his efforts to care for the animals on a train ride to Buenos Aires.

39   Gerald Durrell in *The Whispering Land*

The train journey was not quite as bad as I had anticipated, although, naturally, traveling on an Argentine train with forty-odd cages of assorted livestock is no picnic. My chief fear was that during the night (or day) at some station or other, they would shunt my carriage-load of animals into a siding and forget to reattach it. This awful experience had once happened to an animal-collector friend of mine in South America, and by the time he had discovered his loss and raced back to the station in a hired car, nearly all his specimens were dead. So I was determined that, whenever we stopped, night or day, I was going to be out on the platform to make sure my precious cargo was safe. This extraordinary behavior of leaping out of my bunk in the middle of the night puzzled my sleeping companions considerably. They were three young and charming footballers, returning from Chile where they had been playing. As soon as I explained my actions to them, however, they were full of concern at the amount of sleep I was losing, and insisted on taking turns with me during the night, which they did dutifully during the rest of the trip. To them the whole process must have appeared ludicrous in the extreme, but they treated the matter with great seriousness, and helped me considerably.

Another problem was that I could only get to my animals when the train was in a station, for their van was not connected by the corridor to the rest of the train. Here the sleeping car attendant came into his own. He would warn me ten minutes before we got to a station, and tell me how long we were going to stay there. This gave me time to wend my way down the train until I reached the animal van, and, when the train pulled up, to jump out and minister to their wants.

The three carriages I had to go through to reach the animal van were the third-class parts of the train, and on the wooden benches therein was a solid mass of humanity surrounded by babies, bottles of wine, mothers-in-law, goats, chickens, pigs, baskets of fruit, and other necessities of travel. When this gay, exuberant, garlic-breathing crowd learned the reason for my curious and constant peregrinations * to the van at the back, they united in their efforts to help. As soon as the train stopped they would help me out on to the

* **peregrinations:** journeys.

platform, find the nearest water tap for me, send their children scuttling in all directions to buy the bananas or bread or whatever commodity was needed for the animals, and then, when I had finished my chores, they would hoist me lovingly on board the slowly moving train, and make earnest inquiries as to the puma's health, or how the birds were standing up to the heat. Then they would offer me sweetmeats, sandwiches, glasses of wine or pots of meat, show me their babies, their goats or chickens or pigs, sing songs for me, and generally treat me as one of the family. They were so charming and kind, so friendly, that when we eventually pulled slowly into the huge, echoing station at Buenos Aires, I was almost sorry the trip was over. The animals were piled into a lorry, my hand was wrung by a hundred people, and we roared off to take the creatures, all of whom had survived the journey remarkably well, to join the rest of the collection in the huge shed in the Museum grounds.

The Writer's Craft

1. Very often the personal point of view will be immediately identifiable, because the author's use of "I" and "we" indicates that the narrator is participating directly in the action. Where in this selection do you first realize that the story is being told from a personal point of view? Why is it natural for the author to narrate these events in the first person?

2. In stories told from the personal point of view, the narrator can express his own thoughts and feelings but cannot tell you what is going on in the minds of other participants. Where in this story does Durrell reveal his own thoughts and feelings? The footballers at the end of the first paragraph may have thought Durrell's conduct was ludicrous in the extreme, but the narrator can not be sure. Why not? Does he claim to know what their feelings were?

3. Suppose that the narrative of this overnight train ride had been written from the point of view of the sleeping car attendant. How would it have been different from Durrell's version? Give a brief summary of details and events that might have been included in a narrative written by the attendant.

Write a narrative from a personal point of view describing an experience that taught you something about yourself or another person. In relating the experience, reveal your own thoughts, feelings, and actions. Though you cannot know for sure what other people were thinking on the occasion, you can interpret their thoughts, as Durrell interprets the footballers' thoughts in the model. And you can describe their actions and their expressions. Give a sense of completeness to your narrative by telling about an experience that had a beginning, middle, and end. Include dialogue if possible, and remember to use the personal point of view consistently.

OMNISCIENT POINT OF VIEW   In the following selection the narrator takes no part in the action. The topic — the beginning of a day in Charles Dickens's boyhood — is told from an ominiscient point of view.

40   Rupert Sargent Holland in "Charles Dickens: The Boy of the London Streets"

He was not yet due at the blacking factory, but he hurried away from his room and joined the crowd of early morning people already on their way to work. He went down the embankment along the Thames until he came to a place where a bench was set in a corner of a wall. This was his favorite lounging place. London Bridge was just beyond, the river lay in front of him, and he was far enough away from people to be secure from interruption. As he sat there watching the bridge and the Thames, a small girl came to join him. She was no bigger than he, perhaps a year or two older, but her face was already shrewd enough for that of a grown-up woman. She was the maid of all work at a house in the neighborhood, and she had fallen into the habit of stopping to talk for a few moments with the boy on her way to work in the morning. She liked to listen to his stories. This was his hour for inventing them. He could spin wonderful tales about London Bridge, the Tower, and the wharves along the river. Sometimes he made up stories about the people who passed in front of them, and they were such astonishing stories that the girl remembered them all day as she worked in the house. He seemed to believe them himself; his eyes would grow far away and dreamy and his words would run on and on until a neighboring clock brought him suddenly back to his own position.

The Writer's Craft

1. Stories told from an omniscient point of view give the writer considerable freedom, for he stands outside the narrative, able to enter the minds of all the characters he depicts. What does the author of this model tell you about young Charles Dickens's thoughts and feelings? About the young girl's?

2. The following passage presents the first ten lines of Holland's narrative rewritten from a personal point of view, that of Dickens himself. Compare the effects of the two versions. What different reactions do you have to the personal and omniscient points of view?

> I was not yet due at the blacking factory but hurried away from my room and joined the crowd of early morning people already on their way to work. I went down the embankment along the Thames until I came to a place where a bench was set in a corner of a wall. This was my favorite lounging place; London Bridge was just beyond, the river lay in front of me, and I was far enough away from people to be secure from interruption. As I sat there watching the bridge and the Thames, a small girl came to join me.

Now You Try It

Choose one of the following assignments:

1. Rewrite Durrell's account of the train ride from an omniscient point of view. Because you will be writing from a point of view entirely outside the story, you may include any relevant details and interpretations that will add to the interest of the

narrative. After you have finished, compare the effect of the omniscient version with the original. Try to determine which version you prefer and explain why you prefer it.

2. Write a narrative about an incident you saw or heard about, but in which you did not participate. Maintain an omniscient point of view throughout. Below are suggestions that may give you an idea for your narrative.

a. A heroic deed
b. An incident in a school political campaign
c. An incident seen on your way to or from school
d. An accident
e. An unusual event in your city or home
f. A mob scene
g. An animal's escapades

Sentence Skills

PLACEMENT OF ADVERB PHRASES

37 **Sir Edmund Hillary in "The Summit"** (page 86)

Almost every sentence in the Hillary selection tells of an action. Furthermore, most of the sentences tell *when*, *where*, or *how* the action took place. One way this information is conveyed is through the use of adverb phrases (prepositional phrases that function as adverbs). Notice the italicized adverb phrase in the following sentence from the model:

> We realized that *at this altitude* it might well spell the difference between success and failure.

This adverb phrase is movable, as are many adverbial modifiers, whether single words, phrases, or clauses. It can be placed in different positions within the sentence without damaging the grammatical correctness of the sentence. It is in the middle of Hillary's sentence, but, as shown below, it also could have been placed at the beginning or end:

> *At this altitude* we realized that it might well spell the difference between success and failure.

> We realized that it might well spell the difference between success and failure *at this altitude.*

Compare the three versions of the sentence. Notice that shifting the position of the adverbial modifier creates subtle shifts in emphasis. What is emphasized when the subject and verb of the sentence appear first? when the adverb phrase appears first? when the adverb phrase is in the middle of the sentence? Deciding where to place a movable adverb phrase often depends on the emphasis the writer hopes to achieve within the sentence.

Generally an adverbial modifier is movable when it is not so closely related to the word it modifies that it must remain beside it. In other words, it is movable when it modifies or adds information to the complete statement made in a sentence. The movability of many adverbial modifiers allows the writer to vary the structure of his sentences. If, for example, a paragraph sounds monotonous because too many sentences end with adverbial modifiers, the writer can create a more pleasing effect by putting some of the adverbial modifiers at the beginning and some at the end of sentences. He must, however, be sure that all of his revised sentences read clearly and smoothly. A good way to test placement of modifiers is to read your sentences aloud. If something is wrong with the word order, your ear will detect the flaw and very likely suggest an improved pattern.

■ **EXERCISE A** Move the italicized adverb phrases to all of the other possible positions in the following five sentences from "The Summit," and notice how the emphasis changes. Decide whether shifting the position improved any of the sentences.

1. *After an hour's steady going* we reached the foot of the most formidable looking problem on the ridge — a rock step of some forty feet high.
2. However, *on one occasion* I removed my sunglasses to examine more closely a difficult section of the ridge but was very soon blinded by the fine snow driven by the bitter wind and hastily replaced them.
3. I went on cutting steps *on the narrow strip of snow*.
4. I had been cutting steps continuously *for two hours*, and Tenzing, too, was moving very slowly.
5. I took a firm stance *on the ledge* and signaled to Tenzing to come up.

■ **EXERCISE B** Below are five groups of phrases and clauses, the items in each of which can be combined into a sentence. Each group contains an action verb and one or more adverbial modifiers telling when, where, or how the action took place. Create the strongest and clearest sentences possible by careful placement of the adverbial modifiers. Compare your sentences with those written by your classmates.

1. we managed to climb over the ledge/by noon the next day/after a superhuman effort.
2. he dropped/before anyone could stop him/out of sight/with a terrifying scream

3. without saying a word/hour after hour/on we went
4. we saw the first sign of life/at last/as the sun was setting
5. we covered only twenty miles of rugged terrain/to our great disappointment/on the following day

VARIETY IN THE SIMPLE SENTENCE

38 Frank B. Gilbreth, Jr. and Ernestine Gilbreth Carey in *Cheaper by the Dozen* (page 92)

Having studied grammar, you know that a simple sentence consists of a single independent clause and no subordinate clauses. Though simple sentences are complete if they contain only a subject and a verb or a subject, a verb, and an object, they rarely are that simple. Modifying phrases and compound subjects, verbs, or objects, all used in the construction of simple sentences, let the writer express his ideas fully and also let him produce a pleasing variety in what he writes. To see the variety possible in the simple sentence, examine the following examples from *Cheaper by the Dozen:*

> You could see the Great Experiment hatching in his mind.
>
> The next day he brought home a new, perfectly white typewriter, a gold knife, and an Ingersoll watch.
>
> He unwrapped them and put them on the dining room table.
>
> The knife and watch will be prizes awarded on a handicap basis, taking age into consideration.

In the first sentence a participial phrase *hatching in his mind* modifies "the Great Experiment" and adds information to the sentence. The adverb phrase *the next day* modifies the verb *brought* in the second sentence. Also adding variety are the compound objects *typewriter, knife,* and *watch*. In the third sentence two verbs are used with the same subject: he *unwrapped* and *put*. In addition the adverb phrase *on the dining room table* modifies the verb *put*. The samples here show but a few of the many ways that simple sentences can be made varied and interesting. As you write, you will undoubtedly find other ways to create variety within simple sentences.

■ EXERCISE   Add variety to the simple sentences below by following directions given in parentheses after each sentence.

1. We heard the wind. (Modify *wind* with a participial phrase.)
2. Gerry watched the game. (Add an adverb phrase telling where Gerry watched the game.)
3. I studied before dinner. (Add at least two more verbs telling what was done before dinner so that the sentence has a compound verb.)
4. The waves carved a ledge in the sand. (Modify *waves* with a participial phrase.)
5. The sirens woke the entire neighborhood. (Add a participial phrase modifying *sirens* and an adverb phrase telling when the neighborhood was awakened.)

COORDINATION IN THE COMPOUND SENTENCE

40   Rupert Sargent Holland in "Charles Dickens: The Boy of the London Streets" (page 102)

When a writer wishes to show a close relationship between ideas that are approximately equal in importance, he often constructs a compound sentence. The compound sentence has two or more independent clauses and no subordinate clauses. In such a sentence the writer *coordinates* the ideas he is expressing by putting them into separate independent clauses. He may use a coordinating conjunction to show the relationship between ideas, or, if a coordinating conjunction is unnecessary, he may simply use a semicolon.

Notice how Rupert Sargent Holland has coordinated ideas in the following sentences from the model.

1. He was not yet due at the blacking factory, but he hurried away from his room and joined the crowd of early morning people already on their way to work.
2. She was no bigger than he, perhaps a year or two older, but her face was already shrewd enough for that of a grown-up woman.
3. She was the maid of all work at a house in the neighborhood, and she had fallen into the habit of stopping to talk for a few moments with the boy on her way to work in the morning.

Notice that each independent clause could stand alone as a separate sentence. Notice also that the clauses are joined by coordinating conjunctions. *But* is the coordinating conjunction in sentences 1 and 2. *And* is the coordinating conjunction in sentence 3. Two other coordinating conjunctions, not illustrated here, are *for* and *or*. The functions of these four coordinating conjunctions are as follows:

> *But* contrasts two ideas. (See sentences 1 and 2 above.)
> *And* adds one idea to another. (See sentence 3 above.)
> *For* introduces an idea that is being given as a reason.
> *Or* introduces a result or an alternative idea.

Generally, as in the sentences from the model, a comma is placed before the coordinating conjunction.

■ **EXERCISE** Below are ten pairs of simple sentences. Combine each pair into an effective compound sentence by providing a suitable coordinating conjunction, placing a comma before the conjunction.

1. I have always lived in the city. I think I would like living on a farm.
2. The report cards came out today. I took mine home with leaden feet.
3. I wanted to run away. I was afraid to.
4. The hurricane was moving north. The winds were beginning to hit us.
5. It was difficult to tell what color the uniforms were. Mud covered all the players.
6. Winter is here. Snow covers the ground.
7. The whistle blew. We were off to a running start.
8. Turn the lights out. You will have a large electricity bill.
9. The shutters were closed. The house was deserted.
10. I may decide to go camping. I may stay at home.

SUBORDINATION IN THE COMPLEX SENTENCE

35 Wolcott Gibbs in "Do Re Mi" (page 71)

A sentence consisting of one independent clause and one or more subordinate clauses is called a complex sentence. The independent clause in a complex sentence could stand by itself as a simple sentence. The subordinate clause, however, cannot stand alone, even though it has both a subject and a predicate. The subordinate clause functions within a sentence as an adjective, adverb, or noun. If the subordinate clause modifies a noun or a pronoun, it is an *adjective clause*. If it modifies a verb, an adjective, or an adverb, it is an *adverb clause*. If the subordinate clause functions as a noun, it is a *noun clause*. In the following complex sentence from "Do Re Mi" the two subordinate clauses are italicized.

> We wore little woolly suits and hoods *that gave a sort of startled and bloodthirsty pleasure to the regular students downstairs, who were without our embarrassing advantages.*

In this sentence both subordinate clauses are adjective clauses. The first modifies *suits* and *hoods* by giving information about the effect of this clothing. The second subordinate clause modifies the noun *students*. If the author had not used the subordination in this sentence, he would have had to express all the ideas in independent clauses. The result might have been a series of simple sentences or a compound sentence. To see the difference that subordination makes, compare Gibbs's complex sentence with the two rewritten versions below.

Gibbs's Complex Sentence:

> We wore little woolly suits and hoods that gave a sort of startled and bloodthirsty pleasure to the regular students downstairs, who were without our embarrassing advantages.

Simple sentences:

> We wore little woolly suits and hoods. These suits and hoods gave a sort of startled and bloodthirsty pleasure to the regular students downstairs. Those students were without our embarrassing advantages.

Compound sentence:

> We wore little woolly suits and hoods, and these gave a sort of startled and bloodthirsty pleasure to the regular students downstairs, and they were without our embarrassing advantages.

Which version most clearly expresses the relationship between ideas: Gibbs's complex sentence or one of the rewritten versions?

Now examine another complex sentence from the narrative. Again the subordinate clause is italicized. In this sentence the subordinate clause is an adverb clause; it modifies the verb phrase *lined up.*

> We were lined up in a solemn, woolly row *while one of them wrote a line of strange words on the blackboard.*

Two events are mentioned in the sentence:

1. We were lined up in a solemn woolly row.
2. One of them wrote a line of strange words on the blackboard.

If one of these events had not been subordinated in an adverb clause, would you have understood the relationship in time between the two events? Which word in the complex sentence makes the time relationship clear?

Generally the subordinating conjunction that begins an adverb clause shows the relationship between the independent and the subordinate adverb clause. To verify that statement, try substituting some other subordinating conjunctions (*if, because, after, when, before*) for *while* in Gibbs's sentence, and notice how the different conjunctions change the meaning of the sentence:

> We were lined up in a solemn, woolly row *while* one of them wrote a line of strange words on the blackboard.

■ **EXERCISE** Each group or pair of simple sentences below expresses related ideas. By using subordination, transform each into a complex sentence that shows more clearly the relationship between the ideas. Select one idea to emphasize in an independent clause and subordinate the other ideas to it. Although there may be several ways to combine each group of sentences, you have to show only one of the possible combinations.

Example: I was walking home. I saw a man. He looked familiar. (Use an adverb clause and an adjective clause.)

Rewritten: When I was walking home, I saw a man who looked familiar.

1. The umpire called a foul. The crowd roared its protest. (Use an adverb clause.)

2. Congressman Laughlin recently sponsored a new housing bill. He has represented this district for four years. (Use an adjective clause.)
3. Gary finally mustered enough courage to go out to the end of the diving board. His shaky knees and pounding heart made him turn back. (Use an adverb clause.)
4. I was ten years old. My family traveled through the Southwest and Mexico. (Use an adverb clause.)
5. This is the record. I want to buy it. (Use a noun clause.)
6. She picked up the pieces of the vase. It had shattered on the marble floor. (Use an adjective clause.)
7. The law contains restrictions. They are carefully specified. (Use an adjective clause.)
8. The plants started to wither. They had been left in the sun. I rescued them. (Use an adverb clause and an adjective clause.)
9. The barn burned to the ground. A spark ignited a pile of rags. The rags were saturated with gasoline. (Use an adverb clause and an adjective clause.)
10. The astronauts had been preparing for this flight for two years. They were disappointed. The flight was canceled. (Use an adjective clause and an adverb clause.)

Exposition

LESSON **15**

Organization in Exposition

Exposition is writing that informs or explains: letters, reports, summaries, directions — in short, the kind of writing most of us do most frequently. Often the explanations are brief and simple, as in giving instructions on how to get somewhere. At other times they may be complex, as in explaining a theory or subtle idea. But whether simple or complex, exposition should be organized carefully if it is to be clearly understood.

What is the most effective way to organize exposition? No single answer fits every case. The order in which you present information depends on the material itself and on your purpose in setting it down. Your goal should be to present ideas and facts in as logical an order as you can devise; in so doing, you want to go as far as possible in helping the reader recognize the relationship between individual sentences and paragraphs and between paragraphs and the topic of the composition.

The model in this lesson is an expository passage conveying information about languages. Notice how organization helps make the passage clear.

41   Mario Pei in *What's in a Word?*

[1] Today, there are in existence approximately three thousand separate spoken tongues. Some, like English and Chinese, have hundreds of millions of speakers. Others are spoken by only a few thousand or even a few hundred speakers, like many of ⁵

the native tongues of the North American Indians. Yet each tongue is fully meaningful to its own speakers.

[2] Their differences are enormous, and it is a well-known fact that if the speaker of one language wants to communicate with the speaker of another, he must learn to speak all over again. Yet all languages have certain things in common.

[3] Physically speaking, every language consists of sounds produced by the human vocal organs and received by the human ear. The human vocal organs are capable of producing hundreds, perhaps even thousands of separate sounds, but the average language utilizes only between twenty and sixty of these many possibilities. The fact that they don't all utilize the same sounds complicates matters, because if you have grown used to producing and hearing a certain set of sounds and you are then faced with the need of using another set, your ingrained habits will get in your way.

[4] These sounds are arranged in certain sequences to produce words, as when d-o-g are lined up to give "dog" and c-a-t to give "cat." Here is where agreement among the speakers comes into play. English speakers are agreed that the sequence of three sounds in the spoken word *dog* shall symbolize in their minds the image of a particular animal, and if one speaker utters the word *dog* to another, his listener will automatically receive that image. But that particular sequence of sounds might be altogether meaningless to a speaker of French, whose sound symbol for the animal is *chien*, or to a Spanish speaker, who says *perro*. The situation here is similar to what happens with currencies. My dollar bill is valid for purchases all through the United States, because all Americans have agreed to accept it; but if I go to another country I find that my dollar bills are not legal tender and I have to change them into the currency of that country.

[5] Lastly, the words have to be lined up in accordance with certain traffic rules, which are not

the same in all languages. In English, if I want to indicate more than one dog, I add an -*s* and make "dogs," and my hearer understands that I have more than one dog in mind. Or I may change the order of my words and get a different meaning, in common with my hearer. "John sees George" is one thing. "George sees John" is another.

[6] There is no language that does not have these three things: individual sounds; meaningful sequences of sounds, or words; and traffic rules, such as adding on an ending or arranging the words in certain set sequences.

[7] Learning another language means: (1) acquiring new sounds; (2) learning to accept new sound sequences or words in given meanings; (3) learning new traffic regulations for the new words. Difficult? Yes, but you've done it all before, when you learned your own language. As a baby, you began to hear sounds produced by your parents, and then you tried to imitate them and produce the same sounds. You also learned to associate certain words with certain objects or actions, and to string your words along in a certain way, or make in them certain changes that would modify their meaning. What you did once you can do again.

The Writer's Craft

Introduction

1. The passage is unified around the insight that though languages are numerous and varied, all of them have certain attributes in common. Which paragraph expresses the idea that languages are numerous? Which paragraph introduces the idea that all languages have certain things in common?

Development

2. What three things do all languages have in common? You will find them listed in paragraph 6. In which paragraphs are the three discussed in detail? Is any one of them discussed in more than one of those three paragraphs?

3. Notice that two of the three relevant paragraphs are developed by means of examples. Which one of the three is not? Can you give examples of your own to illustrate the point being made in that paragraph?

Conclusion

4. The insights expressed in paragraphs 3, 4, and 5 and summarized in paragraph 6 lead the author to draw a conclusion that grows logically out of what has gone before. What is the relationship between the common characteristics of all languages and the tasks involved in learning a new language? On what final thought does the author conclude his remarks about the varieties of language and the challenges they pose?

5. To indicate your understanding of the way in which the model has been organized, compose an outline that makes clear what each paragraph contributes to the whole, how it is developed, and how it is related to the paragraphs surrounding.

COHERENCE

1. Transitional expressions link ideas in the passage. What relationship between ideas do the following words indicate?

Yet (lines 7, 12)
But (line 35)
Lastly (line 45)
Or (line 50)

2. Where might the transitional expression "for example" have been reasonably inserted?

3. The writer also uses pronouns to link elements in succeeding sentences. How do the following pronouns in the model help keep the thought flowing smoothly from sentence to sentence? (Hint: Consider the location of their antecedents.)

Some (line 2)
Others (line 4)
they (line 20)

4. How do the following pronoun-and-noun combinations contribute to the coherence of the passage?

Their differences (line 9)
These sounds (line 26)

Now You Try It

Write a composition about one of the topics below, using an organizational plan similar to the one in the model. Before beginning the composition, list the points you plan to include, limiting yourself to three or four that can be explained and illustrated in detail.

Use the first paragraph of the composition to introduce and state your topic clearly. Then devote a separate paragraph to each of the points with which the composition is to be developed. Throughout, use pronouns and transitional expressions so that the reader will be able to follow your train of thought.

a. Nothing is more valuable than a good friend. (Develop by giving characteristics of a good friend.)

b. Teenagers can earn good money these days. (Develop by citing ways for a teenager to earn money.)

c. For me to enjoy it, a movie must fulfill certain requirements. (Develop by giving characteristics of a good movie.)

d. A high-school education provides definite advantages. (Develop by giving advantages of a high-school education.)

LESSON **16**

Explaining a Process

How do you build a boat, study for a test, or paint a fence? How do fluorescent lighting, telephones, or cameras work? What changes take place in plants, animals, and the earth as the seasons change? Answering those questions requires explaining a process, which in turn requires that details be selected carefully and presented as steps in a logical order. The following model explains how the woodchuck hibernates. Notice the way details that have been included are organized.

42   **Alan Devoe in *Lives Around Us***

[1] The woodchuck's hibernation * usually starts about the middle of September. For weeks he has been foraging with increased appetite among the clover blossoms and has grown heavy and slow moving. Now, with the coming of mid-September, apples and corn and yarrow tops have become less plentiful, and the nights are cool. The woodchuck moves with slower gait, and emerges less and less frequently for feeding trips. Layers of fat have accumulated around his chest and shoulders, and there is thick fat in the axils ° of his

* **hibernation:** the inactive state in which many animals spend the winter.
° **axils:** cavities formed where the legs join the body.

legs. He has extended his summer burrow to a length of nearly thirty feet, and has fashioned a deep nest-chamber at the end of it, far below the level of the frost. He has carried in, usually, a little hay. He is ready for the Long Sleep.

[2] When the temperature of the September days falls below fifty degrees or so, the woodchuck becomes too drowsy to come forth from his burrow in the chilly dusk to forage. He remains in the deep nest-chamber, lethargic, hardly moving. Gradually, with the passing of hours or days, his coarse-furred body curls into a semicircle, like a foetus,* nose tip touching tail. The small legs are tucked in, the handlike clawed forefeet folded. The woodchuck has become a compact ball. Presently the temperature of his body begins to fall.

[3] In normal life the woodchuck's temperature, though fluctuant, averages about ninety-seven degrees. Now, as he lies tight-curled in a ball with the winter sleep stealing over him, this body heat drops ten degrees, twenty degrees, thirty. Finally, by the time the snow is on the ground and the woodchuck's winter dormancy has become complete, his temperature is only thirty-eight or forty. With the falling of the body heat there is a slowing of his heartbeat and his respiration. In normal life he breathes thirty or forty times each minute; when he is excited, as many as a hundred times. Now he breathes slower and slower — ten times a minute, five times a minute, once a minute, and at last only ten or twelve times in an hour. His heartbeat is a twentieth of normal. He has entered fully into the oblivion ° of hibernation.

[4] The Long Sleep lasts, on an average, about six months. For half a year the woodchuck remains unmoving, hardly breathing. His pituitary gland is inactive; his blood is so sluggishly circulated that there is an unequal distribution in the chilled body; his sensory awareness has wholly ceased. It is almost true to say that he has altered from a warm-blooded to a cold-blooded animal.

* **foetus:** baby waiting to be born.
° **oblivion:** state of unawareness.

[5] Then, in the middle of March, he wakes. The waking is not a slow and gradual thing, as was the drifting into sleep, but takes place quickly, often in an hour. The body temperature ascends to normal, or rather higher for a while; glandular functions instantly resume; the respiration quickens and steadies at a normal rate. The woodchuck has become himself again, save only that he is a little thinner, and is ready at once to fare forth into the pale spring sunlight and look for grass and berries.

[6] Such is the performance each fall and winter, with varying detail, of bats and worms and bears, and a hundred other kinds of creature. It is a marvel less spectacular than the migration flight of hummingbirds or the flash of shooting stars, but it is not much less remarkable.

The Writer's Craft

1. The introductory paragraph in a composition of this sort usually identifies the process to be explained and often begins the explanation itself. In which sentence does the author name the process he is going to explain? Why is that a logical place in the paragraph to state the topic?

2. The stages of the woodchuck's hibernation that the selection covers are the preparation, the Long Sleep, and the awakening — events that take place in a period of time extending from mid-September to the middle of March. Usually, as is the case here, events in an explanation of a process are presented in chronological order. Why does that order provide an effective way to organize an explanation of a process?

3. Specific details are essential in explaining and describing the various stages in a process. The first paragraph of this selection includes specific details about how the woodchuck prepares for hibernation. We learn that the animal eats a good deal, becomes fat, and moves slowly, and that he extends his burrow to thirty feet and supplies it with a little hay.

Paragraphs 2–4 give information about the period during which the woodchuck is asleep. How, in paragraph 2, is the animal's position in the burrow described? Is the description specific enough to let you visualize the animal as it sleeps? Why, in paragraph 3, do you think the author compares the woodchuck's normal temperature, heartbeat, and respiration with its temperature, heartbeat, and respiration during hibernation? In answering, consider what would have been the effect of not mentioning the normal rates. What details are included in paragraph 4? Do they help complete your understanding of the animal's condition during the Long Sleep?

The woodchuck's awakening is described in paragraph 5. Does the single paragraph provide enough details to make clear what happens in that last stage of the process?

4. Paragraph 6, which concludes the selection, suggests that the author has explained the woodchuck's hibernation as a way of illustrating the wonders of hibernation in general. If the paragraph were omitted, would it alter the effect of the composition as a whole? Discuss.

COHERENCE

1. Transitional expressions help make the order of events clear. List the expressions in paragraphs 2–5 that indicate time order — the sequence of events. *Gradually* and *presently*, from the second paragraph, should appear at the beginning of your list.

2. In addition to transitional expressions, verb tenses help clarify the order of events. In the first paragraph the present perfect tense in the following sentences indicates that the steps mentioned took place before the middle of September:

> For weeks he *has been foraging* with increased appetite . . .
>
> Layers of fat *have accumulated* around his chest and shoulders . . .
>
> He *has extended* his summer burrow to a length of nearly thirty feet, and *has fashioned* a deep nest-chamber at the end of it . . .
>
> He *has carried in*, usually, a little hay.

Which sentences in the first paragraph tell what is happening in the middle of September, the time mentioned at the start? Are all those sentences written in the present tense?

3. Coherence between paragraphs is often achieved by repeating one or more words from the preceding paragraph at the beginning of a new one. Which word in the first sentence of paragraph 3 links it with paragraph 2?

Now You Try It

Choose one of the following assignments:

1. Write a composition explaining a process that you understand thoroughly. Before beginning the composition, list the important stages in the process in chronological order, leaving space under each stage to note specific details you plan to include. Select details that will make the individual steps in the process clear to the reader. When you write your composition, name the process you are explaining in the first paragraph, and present the steps and details in chronological order. Use transitional expressions to indicate time sequence.

The following are some suggested topics.

a. The way a bicycle pump works
b. How a newspaper gets printed and distributed
c. The way your school government functions
d. The making of cloth
e. The transformation of a caterpillar into a butterfly, or a tadpole into a frog
f. The development of a kitten after birth

2. In the "how-to-do-it" explanations that appear frequently in magazines, newspapers, books, and instruction pamphlets, the writer speaks directly to the reader, telling him what to do in each step of a process. As with the Devoe selection, such explanations are organized chronologically.

Write a composition explaining how to do something that you have mastered yourself. If the process requires special equipment, mention it early in the explanation. Present each step in the order in which it should be taken, using transitional expressions wherever necessary to indicate the time sequence. Assume that your reader knows nothing about how to do whatever you are explaining; your directions should be very specific. Listed below are some possible topics:

a. How to paint a room
b. How to make a dress
c. How to mow a lawn
d. How to use a microscope
e. How to make stew
f. How to train a dog to respond to commands

LESSON **17**

Organizing a Comparison

Often comparisons occur in exposition to clarify ideas being explained. The following selection compares Texans and Ukrainians. Notice how the organization helps emphasize similarities between the two peoples and the regions they inhabit — the one in the United States and the other in the Soviet Union.

43   John Fischer in "Ukrainians and Texans"

The Ukrainians are the Texans of Russia. They believe they can fight, drink, ride, sing, and make love better than anybody else in the world, and if pressed will admit it. Their country, too, was a borderland — that's what "Ukraine" means — and like Texas it was originally settled by outlaws, horse thieves, land-hungry farmers, and people who hadn't made a go of it somewhere else. Some of these hard cases banded together, long ago, to raise hell and livestock. They called themselves Cossacks, and they would have felt right at home in any Western movie. Even today the Ukrainians cherish a wistful tradition of horsemanship, although most of them would feel as uncomfortable in a saddle as any Dallas banker. They still like to wear knee-high boots and big, furry hats, made of gray or black Persian lamb, which are the local equivalent of the Stetson.

Even the country looks a good deal like Texas — flat, dry prairie, shading off in the south to semidesert. Through the middle runs a strip of dark, rich soil, the Chernozom Belt, which is almost identical with the black waxy soil of central Texas. It grows the best wheat in the Soviet Union. The Ukraine is also famous for its cattle, sheep, and cotton, and — again like Texas — it has been in the throes of an industrial boom for the last twenty years. On all other people the Ukrainians look with a sort of kindly pity. They might have thought up for their own use the old Western rule of etiquette: "Never ask a man where he comes from. If he's a Texan, he'll tell you; if he's not, don't embarrass him."

The Writer's Craft

1. In making a comparison, a writer has basically two organizational patterns from which to choose. In one, he discusses the subjects of his comparison separately, giving first all the details about one and then all the details about the other. The alternative pattern is based on a point-by-point comparison, which shows how the two subjects are alike or different regarding a number of points in succession. "Ukrainians and Texans" makes a point-by-point comparison. The topic, as stated in the opening sentence, is that Ukrainians are to Russia what Texans are to America. Why is the point-by-point organizational pattern better suited to that topic than the other pattern would have been?

2. On what points does the writer compare Ukrainians and Texans? What points are made about the similarity between Texas and the Ukraine? Does the organization keep the distinction between the people and the land clear? Discuss.

3. An effective comparison avoids unsupported generalities; that is, specific details are included to support the general statements. For example, the second paragraph of the model begins with the assertion that the Ukraine looks like Texas, then provides the specific details that it is "flat, dry prairie, shading off in the south to semidesert." Point out two or three other instances in the model where generalizations are supported with specific details.

Now You Try It

Choose one of the pairs of items listed below, or devise a pair of your own, and write a composition making a point-by-point comparison of the two. Depending on the nature of the items, the points you cover may be similarities, differences, or both. Develop at least three major points of similarity or difference, devoting a separate paragraph to each.

- a. Early explorers of America and today's astronauts
- b. Football and soccer
- c. Character and personality
- d. Westerns and mystery stories
- e. Lake swimming and ocean swimming
- f. Modern buildings and old buildings
- g. New clothing styles and old

LESSON **18**

Description in Exposition

Exposition informs or explains. In the course of doing so, it may make use of descriptive details to clarify a point while appealing to the reader's imagination. As you read the following selection, notice how the author uses description to serve expository ends.

44 Wolfgang Langewiesche
in "What Makes the Weather"

[1] You wake up one morning and you are surprised: the weather, which had been gray and dreary for days and seemed as if it were going to stay that way forever, with no breaks in the clouds and no indication of a gradual clearing, is now all of a sudden clear and sunny and crisp, with a strong northwest wind blowing, and the whole world looks newly washed and newly painted.

[2] "It" has become "fine." Why? How?

[3] Something has cleared the air, you might say. But what? You might study out the weather news in the back of your newspaper, and you would get it explained to you in terms of barometric highs and lows; but just why a rise of barometric pressure should clear the air would still leave you puzzled. The honest truth is that the weather has never been explained. In school they told you about steam engines or electricity or

even about really mysterious things, such as gravitation, and they could do it so that it made sense to a boy. They told you also about the weather, but their explanations failed to explain, and you knew it even then. The lows and highs, cyclones and anticyclones, the winds that blew around in circles — all these things were much more puzzling than the weather itself. That is why weather has always made only the dullest conversation: there simply was no rhyme nor reason to it.

[4] But now there is. A revolutionary fresh view has uncovered the rhyme and reason in the weather. Applied to your particular surprise of that morning, it has this to say:

[5] The air which was warm, moist, and gray last night is still warm, moist, and gray this morning; but it has been pushed fifty or one hundred miles to the south and east of where you live, and has been replaced by a mass of cold, clear, dry air coming from the north or west. It is as simple as that; there is no mysterious "It" in it; just plain physical sense. It is called Air Mass Analysis. . . .

[6] You might inquire next where that morning's new air came from, and just how it got to be cold, dry, and clear. And there you get close to the heart of the new weather science, where meteorology turns into honest, common-sense geography.

[7] That air has come from Canada, where it has been quite literally air-conditioned. Not all parts of the world have the power to condition air, but Canada has. Especially in the fall and winter and early spring, the northern part of this continent becomes an almost perfectly designed mechanical refrigerator. The Rocky Mountains in the west keep currents of new air from flowing into the region. And for weeks the air lies still. The cool ground, much of it snow-covered; the ice of the frozen lakes; plus the perennial stored-up coldness of Hudson's Bay — all cool the layer of air immediately above them. This means a stabilizing and calming of the whole atmosphere all the way up; for cool air is heavy, and with a heavy layer bottommost, there is none of that upflowing of air, that upswelling of mois-

ture-laden heat into the cooler, high altitude which is the mechanism that makes clouds. Thus there may be some low ground fogs there, but above them the long nights of those northern latitudes are clear and starry, wide open toward the black infinite spaces of the universe; and into that black infinity the air gradually radiates whatever warmth it may contain from its previous sojourns over other parts of the world. The result, after weeks of stagnation, is a huge mass of air that is uniformly ice-cold, dry, and clear. It stretches from the Rocky Mountains in the west to Labrador in the east, from the ice wastes of the Arctic to the prairies of Minnesota and North Dakota; and — the third dimension is the most important — it is ice-cold from the ground all the way up to the stratosphere. It is, in short, a veritable glacier of air.

[8] *That* is an air mass. In the jargon of air-faring men, a mass of Polar Canadian air.

[9] When a wave of good, fresh Polar Canadian air sweeps southward into the United States — it happens almost rhythmically every few days — you don't need a barometer to tell you so. There is nothing subtle, theoretical, or scientific about it. You can see and feel the air itself and even hear it. It comes surging out of a blue-green sky across the Dakotas, shaking the hangar doors, whistling in the grass, putting those red-checkered thick woolen jackets on the men, and lighting the stoves in the houses. It flows southward down the Mississippi Valley as a cold wave in winter, or as relief from a heat wave in summer, blowing as a northwest wind with small white hurrying clouds in it. In winter it may sweep southward as far as Tennessee and the Carolinas, bringing frosts with brilliantly clear skies and producing a wave of deaths by pneumonia. Sometimes it even reaches the Texas Gulf Coast; then it is locally called a norther, and the cows at night crowd for warmth around the gas flares in the oil fields. A duck hunter dies of exposure in the coastal swamps. A lively outbreak of Polar Canadian air may reach down into Florida, damage the orange crops, and embarrass local Chambers of Commerce. And

deep outbreaks have been observed to drive all the way down to Central America, where they are feared as a fierce wind called the Tehuantepecer.

[10] Polar Canadian is only one of many sorts of air. To put it in the unprecise language of the layman, the great discovery is that air must always be of some distinct type: that it is never simply air but always conditioned and flavored. What we call weather is caused by gigantic waves in the air ocean which flood whole countries and continents for days at a stretch with one sort of air or another. And there is nothing theoretical about any of these various sorts of air.

[11] Each kind is easily seen and felt and sniffed, and is, in fact, fairly familiar even to the city dweller, although he may not realize it. Each has its own peculiar characteristics, its own warmth or coolness, dampness or dryness, milkiness or clearness. Each has its own quality of light. In each, smoke behaves differently as it pours from the chimneys: in some kinds of air it creeps lazily, in some it bubbles away, in some it floats in layers. That is largely why the connoisseur can distinguish different types of air by smell.

[12] Each type of air combines those qualities into an "atmosphere" of its own. Each makes an entirely different sort of day. In fact, what sort of day it is — raw, oppressive, balmy, dull, a "spring" day — depends almost entirely upon the sort of air that lies over your particular section of the country at that particular time.

[13] And if you tried to describe the day in the old-fashioned terms — wind direction and velocity, humidity, state of the sky — you could never quite express its particular weather; but you can by naming the sort of air. An airplane pilot, once he is trained in the new weather thinking, can get quite impatient with the attempts of novelists, for instance, to describe weather. "Why don't you *say* it was Polar Canadian air and get on with your story?"

[14] And if you are a connoisseur of airs, just about the first thing you will note every morning is something like, "Ah, Caribbean air today"; or if you are

really a judge, you can make statements as detailed as, "Saskatchewan air, slightly flavored by the Great Lakes."

The Writer's Craft

1. The first paragraph of the selection, which introduces the topic, describes a typical, swift change in the weather. What words and phrases describe the "before" and "after" of the weather condition?

2. Although the first paragraph is descriptive, the overall purpose of the selection is soon revealed as expository: to explain why and how weather changes. Where do you become aware that the purpose of the essay is expository? What is the function of the brief second paragraph? Does it provide an effective transition between the introductory paragraph and the body of the composition?

3. In paragraph 5, which initiates the explanation of changes in the weather, the author refers to the situation described at the beginning of the model. What adjectives in the later paragraph describe the departing mass of air? What adjectives describe the new air?

4. In paragraph 7, how are the origins of the cool, dry air explained? Notice that the paragraph makes use of description. The author does not merely state that long nights in northern Canada help cool the air; he includes descriptive details about the nights and the atmosphere:

> . . . the long nights of those northern latitudes are clear and starry, wide open toward the black infinite spaces of the universe; and into that black infinity the air gradually radiates whatever warmth it may contain . . .

Which words and phrases in these lines create a vivid impression?

The final sentence of paragraph 7 states that the air mass coming from northern Canada is "a veritable glacier of air." Why is that an effective way to describe the air?

5. Paragraph 9 asserts that you can see and feel and even hear the Polar Canadian air as it sweeps into the United States. The remainder of the paragraph describes the arrival and some of the effects of the air. Which words and phrases help you see, feel, and hear the air as it flows southward?

6. Paragraph 11 explains that different kinds of air have their own characteristics. What descriptive words and phrases occur in that paragraph?

Now You Try It

Write an expository composition of 300–500 words, using descriptive details in developing your topic. Five topics that call for the use of description are listed below. You may use one of them or supply one of your own, but in either case remember that effective description depends on the use of specific sensory details and precise words.

   a. There are advantages to taking trips by car or bus.
   b. Certain types of clothing unmistakably identify particular occupations.
   c. Facial expressions can be clues to character.
   d. The appearance of a city or town often reflects its history.
   e. This year's _____ is well designed.
   f. Some animals look like people.

EXPOSITION

LESSON **19**

Narration in Exposition

Narratives, usually in the form of brief incidents or anecdotes, are frequently used in expository essays, often to support and illustrate generalizations. Notice in the following selection how the theatrical director Peter Brook supports his general statements by means of a personal narrative.

45   **Peter Brook in "The Immediate Theater"**

[1] A director learns that the growth of rehearsals is a developing process; he sees that there is a right time for everything, and his art is the art of recognizing these moments. He learns that he has no power to transmit certain ideas in the early days. 5
He will come to recognize the look on the face of an apparently relaxed but innerly anxious actor who cannot follow what he is being told. He will then discover that all he needs is to wait, not push too hard. In the third week all will have changed, and 10
a word or a nod will make instant communication. And the director will see that he too does not stay still. However much homework he does, he cannot fully understand a play by himself. Whatever ideas he brings on the first day must evolve continually, 15
thanks to the process he is going through with the actors, so that in the third week he will find that he is understanding everything differently. The actors'

sensibilities turn searchlights on to his own — and he will either know more, or at least see more vividly [20] that he has so far discovered nothing valid.

[2] In fact, the director who comes to the first rehearsal with his script prepared with the moves and business, etc., noted down, is a real deadly theater man. [25]

[3] When Sir Barry Jackson asked me to direct *Love's Labor's Lost* at Stratford in 1945, it was my first big production and I had already done enough work in smaller theaters to know that actors, and above all stage managers, had the greatest contempt [30] for anyone who, as they always put it, "did not know what he wanted." So the night before the first rehearsal I sat agonized in front of a model of the set, aware that further hesitation would soon be fatal, fingering folded pieces of cardboard — forty pieces [35] representing the forty actors to whom the following morning I would have to give orders, definite and clear. Again and again, I staged the very first entry of the Court, recognizing that this was when all would be lost or won, numbering the figures, draw- [40] ing charts, maneuvering the scraps of cardboard to and fro, on and off the set, trying them in big batches, then in small, from the side, from the back, over grass mounds, down steps, knocking them all over with my sleeve, cursing and starting again. As [45] I did so, I noted the moves, and with no one to notice my indecision, crossed them out, then made fresh notes. The next morning I arrived at rehearsal, a fat promptbook under my arm, and the stage management brought me a table, reacting to my volume, [50] I observed, with respect.

[4] I divided the cast into groups, gave them numbers, and sent them to their starting places; then, reading out my orders in a loud confident way, I let loose the first stage of the mass entrance. As the [55] actors began to move I knew it was no good. These were not remotely like my cardboard figures, these large human beings thrusting themselves forward, some too fast with lively steps I had not foreseen,

bringing them suddenly on top of me — not stop- [60]
ping, but wanting to go on, staring me in the face:
or else lingering, pausing, even turning back with
elegant affectations that took me by surprise. We
had only done the first stage of the movement, letter A on my chart, but already no one was rightly [65]
placed and movement B could not follow. My heart
sank and, despite all my preparation, I felt quite
lost. Was I to start again, drilling these actors so
that they conformed to my notes? One inner voice
prompted me to do so, but another pointed out that [70]
my pattern was much less interesting than this new
pattern that was unfolding in front of me — rich in
energy, full of personal variations, shaped by individual enthusiasms and lazinesses, promising such
different rhythms, opening so many unexpected pos- [75]
sibilities. It was a moment of panic. I think, looking
back, that my whole future work hung in the bal-
ance. I stopped, and walked away from my book, in
amongst the actors, and I have never looked at a
written plan since. I recognized once and for all the [80]
presumption and the folly of thinking that an inani-
mate model can stand for a man.

The Writer's Craft

1. Instead of including a personal narrative in paragraphs 3
and 4, the author might have conveyed the same idea through
straight exposition:

> What makes such a director deadly? Mostly it is because
> he will not be in a position to respond imaginatively to
> what is bound to happen as rehearsals get underway — to
> the personal variations, individual enthusiasms and lazi-
> nesses of the actors that promise such different rhythms
> and open so many unexpected possibilities. To be sure,
> every director realizes that actors and stage managers are
> contemptuous of anyone who, as they always put it, "don't
> know what he wants." But even so, a director's understand-
> able desire to give his actors orders that are definite and
> clear should not betray him into making the mistake of ar-

riving at rehearsal with a fat promptbook under his arm and each move of every actor in the play planned out in detail and written down.

Compare the expository paragraph above with Brook's two narrative paragraphs. Which is more effective? Give reasons for your answer.

2. As you noticed in models 14 and 15, in the lesson on paragraph development, narrative anecdotes provide effective support for generalizations made in expository paragraphs. What are some of the advantages of including brief supporting narratives in expository essays?

COHERENCE

1. One way to gain coherence is through the use of parallel structure, which helps make clear the relationship between similar ideas. The second sentence of the model begins, "He learns that. . . ." The third and fourth begin in very similar ways: "He will come to recognize . . ."; "He will then discover that. . . ." What is the relationship between the three sentences made parallel in that way?

2. Later in the same paragraph two more sentences are related closely to each other through parallel structure; both begin with quite similar subordinate clauses. Which sentences are they?

WORD CHOICE: EXPRESSING AN ATTITUDE

An author's attitude toward his subject is conveyed in part through the words that he chooses to express his meaning. "He was thrifty" conveys a different attitude from "He was stingy." A girl might look slender to one person and skinny to another, depending on their contrasting attitudes toward her. What attitude is conveyed by these words from the model taken together in context: *contempt* (line 30), *agonized* (line 33), *fatal* (line 34)? Suppose the sentences in which those words appear had been written:

> . . . I had already done enough work in smaller theaters to know that actors, and above all stage managers, were not at ease with anyone who, as they always put it, "did not know what he wanted." So the night before the first rehearsal I had a look at a model of the set, aware that further hesitation might cause me some embarrassment. . . .

How do the alterations change the author's attitude toward what he is saying?

2. Notice the attitude conveyed by the following italicized words:

> As the actors began to move I knew it was *no good*. These were not *remotely* like my cardboard figures, these *large* human beings *thrusting* themselves forward. . . .

What is the author's attitude toward what he is describing? How would that attitude be changed if the sentence were rewritten to read:

> As the actors began to move I knew it wasn't quite right. These were not the same as my cardboard figures, these people coming forward. . . .

Now You Try It

Use brief narratives as aids to giving information about one of the topics suggested below or a topic of your own choice. You may use narration in your composition either to introduce your topic or to illustrate the generalizations you make in the development of the composition. In either case, the narrative will most likely take the form of an incident or personal anecdote. In writing, try to choose words that effectively reflect your attitude toward your topic.

a. Teenagers have their own slang.
b. High spirits can get you in trouble.
c. Teamwork is the key to winning.
d. It takes more than a cookbook to guarantee success in the kitchen.
e. TV Westerns generally follow the same pattern in both plot and characterization.
f. Literature can be a key to understanding others.
g. The antics of _____ always tickle my funny bone. (Name the comedian.)
h. A hobby can be profitable.
i. A quarterback must be able to make decisions quickly.
j. Trips with the family may be both pleasurable and painful.
k. "The squeaky axle gets the grease."

LESSON **20**

Analogy in Exposition

Sometimes the most effective way to clarify an unfamiliar or abstract idea is by comparing it with something the reader is likely to know. Mark Twain uses that kind of comparison — or analogy, as it is called — in the following expository paragraphs from *Life on the Mississippi.*

46   Mark Twain in *Life on the Mississippi*

There is one faculty which a pilot * must incessantly cultivate until he has brought it to absolute perfection. Nothing short of perfection will do. That faculty is memory. He cannot stop with merely thinking a thing is so and so; he must know it; for this is eminently one of the "exact" sciences. With what scorn a pilot was looked upon, in the old times, if he ever ventured to deal in that feeble phrase "I think" instead of the vigorous one "I know!"

One cannot easily realize what a tremendous thing it is to know every trivial detail of twelve hundred miles of river, and know it with absolute exactness. If you will take the longest street in New York and travel up and down it, conning ° its features patiently until you know every house and window and lamppost and

---

* **pilot:** a river pilot.
° **conning:** studying.

big and little sign by heart, and know them so accurately that you can instantly name the one you are abreast of when you are set down at random in that street in the middle of an inky-black night, you will then have a tolerable notion of the amount and the exactness of a pilot's knowledge who carries the Mississippi River in his head. And then, if you will go on until you know every street crossing, the character, size, and position of the crossing stones, and the varying depth of mud in each of these numberless places, you will have some idea of what the pilot must know in order to keep a Mississippi steamer out of trouble. Next, if you will take half of the signs in that long street and change their places once a month, and still manage to know their new positions accurately on dark nights, and keep up with those repeated changes without making mistakes, you will understand what is required of a pilot's peerless memory by the fickle Mississippi.

The Writer's Craft

1. The selection begins by asserting that a river pilot should have a perfect memory in order to keep every detail of the Mississippi in mind. To demonstrate the difficulty of knowing the river thoroughly, the author makes an analogy. To what does he compare the river? Is the comparison effective? Explain.

2. Mark Twain emphasizes three aspects of what a river pilot needs to know. First, he must know every detail of the 1,200 miles of the river. Second, he must know all the problems of navigation in order to keep a steamer out of trouble. Finally, he must be able to recognize and then remember all the changes in the river. How is the analogy used to emphasize the difficulties involved in each of those tasks?

The following selection is taken from an article about advertising and its effect on the American consumer, the three paragraphs given here being the writer's introduction to his topic. Notice how an analogy helps clarify his position.

47   Robert Graham in "Adman's Nightmare"

[1] Advertisements are all like tacks placed in the road, and the mind of the American consumer is somewhat like an automobile tire. The outer layers of the tire, made of black, smoke-cured apathy, are resilient and hard to pierce. But a good sharp tack can do it, and a superior tack can go on and puncture the inner tube. When that happens, the consumer comes to a shuddering halt and the man who put the tack in the road, or hired somebody else to do it for him, steps out of the bushes and sells the consumer an icebox. There is nothing wrong with this — most of the time the consumer needs the icebox anyway, and in buying it he performs a function vital to the operation of the economy.

[2] Advertisers are very good at making tacks. They can make big sharp ones — the concept of mildness, for example, has lacerated countless tires in its time. They can make medium-sized tacks — the celebrity testimonial is an example of that sort, standard and solid, likely to cause some punctures but not guaranteed to work every time. Or the advertisers can make little tacks like the singing commercial, one of which may not make much of a dent, but which can be effective in large numbers when strewn across the consumer's road.

[3] The consumer is familiar with all the standard varieties of tacks. But just now, no farther away than the nearest radio or television set or the very pages he is about to read, a new and different sort awaits him. Since the war, and particularly during the past year, advertisers have been devoting new attention to the questions of what makes the tire so tough and whether there is another, easier means of puncturing it. They are discovering that there is indeed an easier means, and that there are some technicians, or needlers, who are very familiar with it. The means is psychology, and the needlers are known collectively as social scientists — sociologists, anthropologists, and psychologists.

The Writer's Craft

1. What purpose does the tack-and-tire analogy serve? In your answer, consider how the analogy dramatizes the effect of advertisements and also creates interest in the writer's statements about the way advertising works. In paragraph 2, for example, how does the writer use the analogy to describe three different kinds of advertisements?

2. How is the tack-and-tire analogy used in paragraph 3? What purpose or purposes does it serve there?

Now You Try It

Select one of the following assignments:

1. Explain the process of solving a mystery by comparing it to putting together a jigsaw puzzle.

2. Describe the changes in your moods by comparing them to changes in the seasons.

3. Explain the way a person learns a foreign language by comparing the process to the way skill is acquired in a specific sport.

4. Describe an unimaginative person by comparing him to a robot or computer.

5. Use an analogy in a composition developing one of the following topics or a topic of your own choice.

   a. The difficulty of making and keeping a friend
   b. The way political elections work
   c. How planes fly
   d. The desire to explore outer space
   e. The pleasures of a vacation
   f. The ingredients of academic success
   g. The benefits of a good education
   h. The appeal of a particular sport

Sentence Skills

VARIETY IN SENTENCE BEGINNINGS

42   Alan Devoe in *Lives Around Us* (page 120)

Although the normal word order in an English sentence is subject, verb, object, you do not have to make the subject the first word in every sentence. Modifiers, especially adverbial modifiers, can be used to begin sentences, thereby adding interest and variety to your writing. Notice the different ways sentences begin in the following paragraph from the Devoe selection. Three of the five begin with something other than the subject.

> When the temperature of the September days falls below fifty degrees or so, the woodchuck becomes too drowsy to come forth from his burrow in the chilly dusk to forage. He remains in the deep nest-chamber, lethargic, hardly moving. Gradually, with the passing of hours or days, his coarse-furred body curls into a semicircle, like a foetus, nose tip touching tail. The small legs are tucked in, the handlike clawed forefeet folded. The woodchuck has become a compact ball. Presently the temperature of his body begins to fall.

Sentence 1 begins with an adverb clause; sentence 3, with an adverb and an adverb phrase; sentence 5, with an adverb. Sentences 2 and 4 begin with their subjects.

Reread the eight sentences that make up paragraph 3 of Alan Devoe's *Lives Around Us* on page 121. How many begin with their subjects? How do the others begin?

■ **EXERCISE**   All the sentences in the paragraph below begin with the subject. Rewrite the paragraph so that some start with an adverbial modifier. Begin with a single word, a phrase, or a clause. You may add and change words, rearrange the parts within a sentence, and combine sentences.

But do not change every sentence; your final paragraph should contain a few sentences that begin with the subject.

Charles Lindbergh made the first transatlantic plane flight in May 1927, and he became a public hero. He arrived in Paris after a flight of thirty-three hours, and he was greeted by wild crowds. He had succeeded in doing what a pair of French fliers, Nungesser and Coli, had failed to do. The President of the French Republic, to show the gratitude and thoughtfulness of the French people, gave Lindbergh a medal. He immediately became an ambassador of good will as well as a hero. Kings and queens, dukes and princes, and the common people of Belgium and England lined the streets to pay tributes of admiration and affection. He returned soon to the United States. He was acclaimed and honored by both the President and the American people.

PARALLEL STRUCTURE FOR IDEAS OF EQUAL IMPORTANCE

**44 Wolfgang Langewiesche
in "What Makes the Weather" (page 128)**

Parallel ideas should be expressed in the same grammatical form. The sentence, "I like swimming and to fish" is awkward, because *swimming* is a gerund, and *to fish* is an infinitive. That is, they are not parallel. Notice how much smoother and clearer sentences using parallel grammatical forms are: "I like swimming and fishing" or "I like to swim and to fish."

In the three sentences that follow, from "What Makes the Weather," parallel forms are italicized.

You can *see* and *feel* the air itself and even *hear* it.

This means a *stabilizing* and *calming* of the whole atmosphere all the way up.

It stretches *from the Rocky mountains in the west to Labrador in the east, from the ice wastes of the Arctic to the prairies of Minnesota and North Dakota.*

In the first sentence, three *verbs* tell how you can experience the air. What grammatical form is repeated in the second sentence? In the third sentence?

Parallel structure not only makes writing clearer but also helps make it concise. The following sentence, also from the model, describes five different actions of the wind in parallel participial phrases.

> It comes *surging out of a blue-green sky across the Dakotas, shaking the hangar doors, whistling in the grass, putting those red-checkered thick woolen jackets on the men, and lighting the stoves in the houses.*

Without the use of parallel structure, a separate sentence might have been required to describe each action, perhaps as follows:

> It comes surging out of a blue-green sky across the Dakotas. It shakes the hangar doors. It whistles in the grass. It puts those red-checkered thick woolen jackets on the men. It lights the stoves in the houses.

The ideas are the same, but the expression is not so concise as is the original sentence.

■ **EXERCISE** Complete each of the following sentences with at least two grammatically parallel words, phrases, or clauses.

1. My hobby helps me ————. (Use infinitive phrases.)
2. The rain falls ————. (Use participial phrases.)
3. At this time of year students are ————. (Use adjectives.)
4. ———— are some of the ways teenagers can earn money. (Use gerund phrases.)
5. An investigation of the crime revealed ————. (Use noun clauses beginning with "that.")

THE ADJECTIVE CLAUSE

**45 Peter Brook
in "The Immediate Theater"** (page 134)

As you know, a complex sentence is made up of an independent clause and one or more subordinate clauses. One kind of subordinate clause is the adjective clause, modifying a noun or pronoun in a complex sentence. In the following example from "The Immediate Theater," the adjective clause is italicized.

He will come to recognize the look on the face of an apparently relaxed but innerly anxious actor *who cannot follow what he is being told.*

The ideas expressed in the complex sentence can be stated in two simple sentences:

He will come to recognize the look on the face of an apparently relaxed but innerly anxious actor. The actor cannot follow what he is being told.

Do you understand as clearly the relationship between ideas in the two simple sentences? Do the two read as smoothly as the single complex sentence?

Now look at these sentences from "The Immediate Theater":

In fact, the director *who comes to the first rehearsal with his script prepared with the moves and business, etc., noted down,* is a real deadly theater man.

When Sir Barry Jackson asked me to direct *Love's Labor's Lost* at Stratford in 1945, it was my first big production and I had already done enough work in smaller theaters to know that actors, and above all stage managers, had the greatest contempt for anyone *who, as they always put it, "did not know what he wanted."*

One inner voice prompted me to do so, but another pointed out that my pattern was much less interesting than this new pattern *that was unfolding in front of me — rich in energy, full of personal variations, shaped by individual enthusiasms and lazinesses, promising such different rhythms, opening so many unexpected possibilities.*

On the basis of the sentences, answer the following questions:

1. What is the usual position of the adjective clause in relation to the noun it modifies? Is it possible to rearrange the parts of the sentence so that the adjective clause comes before the word it modifies?
2. What words introduce the adjective clauses in these sentences? Do those introductory words help relate the two parts of the sentence? (Other words that introduce adjective clauses are *whose, whom, which,* and sometimes *where.*)

Notice the different ways of punctuating the two adjective clauses in the following sentence:

> *Love's Labor's Lost*, which is a comedy by William Shakespeare, was the first big production that Peter Brook directed.

A comma precedes and follows the first adjective clause ("which is a comedy by William Shakespeare") because it is not essential to the meaning of the sentence. Omitting it does not basically alter what the sentence conveys: "*Love's Labor's Lost* was the first big production that Peter Brook directed." A comma does not set off the second clause, however; that clause is vital and cannot be omitted. It makes no sense to say "*Love's Labor's Lost*, which is a comedy by William Shakespeare, was the first big production."

The examples illustrate the rules for punctuating adjective clauses. With a nonessential clause use commas. Do not use them when the clause is essential.

■ **EXERCISE** Combine the following sets of simple sentences into one complex sentence by changing one of the sentences into an adjective clause. Set the clause off with commas if it is *not* essential to the meaning of the sentence.

1. During our trip through Virginia, we visited Monticello. Monticello was the home of Thomas Jefferson.
2. The boys skipped gym class. They were kept after school.
3. The bank shows the influence of Greek architecture. It has large pillars across the front.
4. The strings of colored lights hanging across the main street are an indication. The holidays are near.
5. This town is made up of empty houses and dusty streets. Once it was a prosperous gold-mining center.

Opinion and Persuasion

LESSON **21**

Supporting an Opinion

What do you like? What do you think of it? Which do you prefer? Answering such questions means stating opinions, any one of which may serve as the topic of an essay. Examples, facts, and incidents all may provide effective means of supporting the opinion and thus developing the composition. Incidentally, skills of expository writing play their part here, too, even though the writer's purpose in an essay of opinion differs from his purpose in exposition. Exposition informs or explains, whereas an essay of opinion seeks to convince or persuade. In the latter instance, the author may sometimes simply want to convince the reader of the soundness of a particular opinion; at other times he may hope to persuade the reader to change his mind.

The following passage expresses an opinion about the merit of canoes. Observe how effectively the opinion is supported.

48   David Klein in "Canoes"

[1] If you have ever ridden a fine English bicycle after being accustomed to a heavyweight American model, you will have some notion of what your first few minutes in a canoe will feel like. The lightness, the maneuverability, the distance that you can cover

with a single, easy stroke of a paddle will make you feel that every other boat you've ever used was a coal barge by comparison. In recent years the canoe has lost popularity to the more fashionable outboard motorboat and sailboat; but, if you are willing to make your own decisions instead of following the crowd, you may well find that the canoe is not only "the most boat for the money" but also the perfect boat for you.

[2] New or used, a canoe costs relatively little and has a long life. A new canoe costs about as much as a low-priced outboard hull (without motor). Properly cared for, it can last thirty years or more, and if you get tired of it, you can sell it for a fairly large fraction of its original cost. A used canoe — especially if it needs a patch or some other minor repairs that seem to be too much of a job for the present owner — can often be bought for a few dollars, and sometimes can be picked up for the asking.

[3] But low price is only one of the canoe's advantages — and not necessarily the greatest. More important is the fact that its light weight makes it the most easily portable boat available. You can carry it on a car top without the need for a trailer, or you can ship it by truck at no great expense. Its light weight and its construction eliminate storage problems. During the summer a pair of saw horses or even a couple of boards near the water's edge take the place of the usual mooring, and from here you can launch the canoe and be aboard and away in minutes instead of going through the lengthy preparation that a larger boat demands. In the winter you can store the canoe on the rafters of the garage or even in the basement or the attic.

[4] The canoe's design fits it for almost any sort of water and any sort of use. Because it draws * only three to six inches fully loaded, you can use it in anything larger than a respectable rain puddle, and you can take it into marshes and down shoal rivers that are unnavigable by any other craft. Because a canoe is

* **draws:** requires for floating.

portageable, dams and canal locks won't make you change your itinerary. And in many parts of the country you can cruise for hundreds of miles by carrying the canoe and your gear a few hundred feet from one lake or river to another.

[5] Many boats are designed either for cruising or for one-day trips, but the canoe is suited to both. For a short run after school or on a weekend, you can simply toss a paddle and a couple of cushions aboard and go off with a friend or by yourself, without any sort of preparation. But the same boat will take you and your friend and all your camping equipment, cooking gear, and supplies off on a two- or three-week cruise and will even serve as a shelter when you spend the night ashore.

The Writer's Craft

1. Addressed to readers who may wish to buy a boat, the selection presents advantages of the canoe over other kinds of water craft. The author's overall opinion of canoes is made clear in the final sentence of the first paragraph:

> . . . you may well find that *the canoe is not only "the most boat for the money" but also the perfect boat for you.*

What purpose do the first two sentences in the essay have? Do they help create an effective introductory paragraph? Explain.

2. Paragraph 2 offers support for the opinion that the canoe is "the most boat for the money." The first advantages mentioned are the low cost and long life of a canoe. Notice that the first sentence in paragraph 2 is a topic sentence. How is it supported? Are enough specific details given to make the general statement convincing?

3. What advantages of the canoe are cited in paragraphs 3, 4, and 5? In each instance a general statement about the advantage is supported by means of specific details. Why is that pattern an effective one to follow in an essay of opinion? How would the reader react if the writer simply supported his overall opinion with a series of generalizations?

The following essay of opinion tells what one person thinks of the comics and why.

49   John Mason Brown in "I Hate the Comics"

[1] I love comedians, the highest and the lowest. I love cartoons, too. My allergy to comics, however, is complete, utter, absolute. I know there are bad comics, and I presume there are good comics. I have read a few of both — under protest. But I regret them both. I deplore them. And, to continue the understatement, I abhor them. So far as I am concerned, they might just as well be written in a foreign language for which no dictionary has ever been published. I wish they had been.

[2] Let me quickly admit that I am low enough, and sometimes defeated enough, as a parent, to make use of comics. I mean in desperate moments when, of a rainy Sunday morning or afternoon, I want peace in the home. Or when I am traveling with my two sons on a train and need to subdue them. Then — yes, I'll confess it — then I do resort to comics. Without shame, without conscience. On such occasions I don't so much *distribute* comics as I *administer* them to my sons. Much as a doctor would employ a hypodermic. As knockout drops for unruly children, as sedatives, as maxim silencers,* comics do have their undeniable uses. This much I'll concede, gratefully.

[3] I'll also grant that so long as other people's children read comics we have scant hope, and perhaps less right, to keep our own from doing so. It would be unfair for us to deny to our children what is now a group experience and, when they have grown up, will have become a group memory of their generation.

[4] If I hate the comics, I have my reasons. I know that, as part of a healthy diet, everyone needs a certain amount of trash. Each generation has always found its own trash. I doubt if our grandfathers were harmed by the dime novels about Kit Carson, Jesse

---

* **maxim silencers:** silencers for firearms, named for the inventor Hiram Percy Maxim.

James, etc., on which they fed. I doubt, too, if Little Nemo, Mutt and Jeff, Foxy Grandpa, Buster Brown, or the Katzenjammer Kids did serious damage to those of my vintage when we read them once a week.

[5] Give me Henty, *The Rover Boys, The Motor Boys,* or *Tom Swift on the Mississippi,* or any books written in words for those who can read, any day in preference to the comic books. The comic books, however, as they are nowadays perpetually on tap, seem to me to be, not only trash, but the lowest, most despicable, and most harmful form of trash. As a rule, their word selection is as wretched as their drawing, or the paper on which they are printed. They are designed for readers who are too lazy to read, and increase both their unwillingness and inability to do so.

[6] I won't and can't deny that comic books fascinate the young as, in terms of pigs, rabbits, rodents, morons, hillbillies, and supermen, they tell their illustrated stories. But, as a writer, I resent the way in which they get along with the poorest kind of writing. I hate their lack of both style and ethics. I hate their appeal to illiteracy and their bad grammar. I loathe their tiresome toughness, their cheap thrills, their imbecilic laughter.

[7] I despise them for making only the story count and not the *how* of its telling. I detest them, in spite of their alleged thrills and gags, because they have no subtlety and certainly no beauty. Their power of seduction, I believe, lies in the fact that they make everything too easy. They substitute bad drawing for good description. They reduce the wonders of the language to crude monosyllables, and narratives to no more than printed motion pictures.

[8] What riles me when I see my children absorbed by the comics is my awareness of what they are not reading, and could be reading; in other words, my awareness of the more genuine and deeper pleasures they could be having. To compare Bugs Bunny or Donald Duck with *The Jungle Book* or even *The Travels of Babar;* to set Wanda, the Wonder Woman, against *Alice in Wonderland,* or Batman and Robin,

Dick Tracy, and Gene Autry against *Treasure Island,* Li'l Abner against *Huck Finn* or *Tom Sawyer,* or Superman and Captain Marvel against Jules Verne or *Gulliver's Travels,* is to realize that, between the modern cave drawing (which a comic book is) and a real book, a good book, there is — to put it mildly — a difference. A tragic difference, which is hard on the young and may be harder on the future.

[9] Anatole France once described even the best books as being "the opium of the Occident." Well, most comics, as I see them, are the bane of the bassinet; the horror of the house; the curse of the kids; and a threat to the future. They offer final and melancholy proof that, even among the young, the mind is the most unused muscle in the United States.

[10] I don't care how popular comics are with the young or, worse still, with the old. They seem to me to be sad proofs of arrested underdevelopment. Time in the modern world is no longer something to be wasted. The moment has overtaken us, whether we like it or not, and most of us do not, when as a people we must grow up. In order to grow up, we must put behind us that fear of the best and that passion for the mediocre which most Americans cultivate.

The Writer's Craft

1. Is the author's opinion of the comics expressed clearly and forcefully in the first paragraph?

2. The author establishes early that he is not opposed to all kinds of humor. Where in the first paragraph does he assure the reader that he does like some forms of humor? Why would you suppose he feels such assurance is necessary?

3. Before presenting his reasons for hating the comics, Brown grants two advantages they may possibly possess. Knowing that many of his readers will be parents who use comics to keep their children quiet, he admits in paragraph 2 that he also uses them for that purpose. What other reason for permitting children to read comic books is acknowledged in paragraph 3?

4. Paragraphs 4–9 support and develop the author's opinion of the comics. What reasons are given to justify that opinion? In other words, what does the author feel is wrong with comics in terms of their content and their effect on the reader's mind?

5. Notice the parallel grammatical constructions in these consecutive sentences from paragraph 6:

> I hate their lack of both style and ethics.
> I hate their appeal to illiteracy and their bad grammar.
> I loathe their tiresome toughness, their cheap thrills, their imbecilic laughter.

Does the parallelism help emphasize the writer's feelings about comic books? Why, or why not?

6. In the following extracts from the model the same idea is repeated in different words several times within the same sentence. (Repeated elements are italicized.) What effect do the repetitions have? For example, do they help emphasize the writer's opinions?

> My allergy to comics, however, is *complete, utter, absolute.*
> *As knockout drops for unruly children, as sedatives, as maxim silencers,* comics do have their undeniable uses.
> The comic books . . . seem to me to be, not only trash, but the *lowest, most despicable,* and *most harmful form of trash.*
> Well, most comics, as I see them, are *the bane of the bassinet; the horror of the house; the curse of the kids;* and *a threat to the future.*

7. An effective way to conclude an essay of opinion is by restating and summarizing the views developed earlier. How does the final paragraph of this selection summarize the author's views on comics? Does it also suggest that Brown is writing not just to express his own opinion but to affect the reader's attitude as well?

WORD CHOICE: SYNONYMS

This opinion of the comics makes use of many synonyms for the verb *hate*. In the first paragraph, the author says that he *regrets, deplores,* and *abhors* the comics. Find two more synonyms for *hate* in paragraph 6 and two in paragraph 7. What is the effect of using synonyms instead of repeating the verb *hate*?

Now You Try It

Choose one of the following assignments:

1. John Mason Brown expressed this opinion of comics in 1946; since then, of course, many new comics have appeared. Consider your own opinion of current comics. Do you like or dislike them? Write an essay of 250–300 words expressing and supporting that opinion; develop the essay by mentioning specific comics, and support your generalizations with specific details.

2. Write an essay of opinion stating that something is the best or worst of its kind. You may want to write about a particular book, movie, television show, kind of music, or sport. After stating your opinion in the introductory paragraph, develop the essay by giving specific reasons that support it in succeeding paragraphs. Conclude with a paragraph summarizing your views.

LESSON **22**

Using Examples
to Support an Opinion

If a writer wants his opinion to be taken seriously, he must support it with evidence. The author of the following essay has an opinion about the way Americans fill their leisure time, and he supports it with evidence in the form of examples.

50   **Russell Baker
in "The Paradox * of the New Leisure"**

With the onset of the vacation season the real problem of the new leisure becomes obvious. Leisure pastime in this country has become so complicated that it is now hard work.

Golf is a case in point. A big thing to do with ⁵
leisure time is to golf it away. All well and good for those who grew up next door to the golf links, but what of the millions who wasted their muscular years working up to golfing status and now come to the game unable to tell a five-iron from a backhand? ¹⁰

It is impossible for them to drop by a golf course, borrow somebody's clubs, and start swinging away. Even on most public courses one needs an appoint-

* **paradox:** contradictory qualities.

ment to tee off, and people who hate making fools
of themselves in public often need instruction from ¹⁵
a professor.

To golf in style – and style is almost everything
in the new leisure – a club membership is *de
rigueur*.* A golf wardrobe has to be bought. Clubs,
too. And people who hate making fools of themselves ²⁰
before golf-club salesmen will need preliminary instruction in the difference between a mashie and a
niblick, if that is what they are called.

Fishing is worse. The party who remembers fishing as a time killer performed along creek banks ²⁵
with a length of twine, a beanpole, ten cents' worth
of hooks, and a can of worms is in for deep shock at
the sporting-goods shop today.

First off, the salesman wants to know what kind
of fishing he means to do. Like everything else, to- ³⁰
day's fishing is for specialists. Admit that you want
to put worms on a hook and angle for sunfish and
they will rise from their spinners, flies, and four-ply
nylon coelacanth casting line and laugh you out of
existence. ³⁵

Modern fishing is as complicated as flying a B-58
to Tacoma. Several years of preliminary library and
desk work are essential just to be able to buy equipment without humiliation.

Sailing is another popular time killer, though it ⁴⁰
is hard to see why, considering all the study and
labor it involves. In the first place, it means buying
a boat, then finding some place to keep the thing,
then finding someone to explain the difference between tacking and keelhauling. ⁴⁵

It is also dangerous. Tack when you should be
keelhauling, and it may be the end of the new leisure.

People who fear proving themselves inadequate
at golf, fishing, and sailing may, of course, devote ⁵⁰
themselves to the passive culture, music, for example. They soon discover, however, that harmoniz-
ing the soul with Berlioz isn't so easy.

* *de rigueur:* French phrase meaning "necessary for good form."

The day when a man bought a phonograph, put
Berlioz on the turntable, and opened a beer is past. [55]
Nowadays he must buy a sound system. It comes in
thousands of small electronic parts which must be
assembled according to directions in Assyrian.

The object is for each man to build a personal
system which will produce a Berlioz purer than any [60]
man in the neighborhood has ever heard. The be-
ginner invariably gets his woofer * crossed with
his mashie, which produces spinnaker feedback,
resulting in excessive bassoon tweeter ° in the book-
case. [65]

After ruining his first system, the music culturist
usually sees the wisdom of a four-year course at the
Massachusetts Institute of Technology. This suggests
that the sociologists who have been worrying that
the decline of work and the increase of leisure may [70]
ruin us have been jousting with a straw man.

With its genius for self-adjustment, the society
has turned leisure into labor. We are not far from
the time when a man after a hard weekend of leisure
will go thankfully off to his job to unwind. [75]

* **woofer:** a loudspeaker that reproduces low-pitch sounds.
° **tweeter:** a loudspeaker that reproduces high-pitch sounds.

The Writer's Craft

1. The essay begins with an opinion about the use of leisure
time in America. What is that opinion?

2. To support the opinion, the author cites four leisure-time
activities as examples. What four examples are given? Make a
brief outline showing how those examples contribute to the organizational plan of the selection.

3. The author is not content simply to say that the four activities are complicated; he mentions specific difficulties related
to each activity. With what details does he demonstrate the com-
plexities of golfing? of fishing? of sailing? of music? Which details
do you feel offer the most convincing support for the initial statement of opinion?

4. Each example of an activity supports the writer's opinion,
yet each is a separate part of the essay. The selection is coherent

because the relationship between the specific examples and the general topic, as well as that between the individual examples themselves, is clear. How are the links that show those relationships supplied? In answering, cite specific words and phrases wherever possible.

5. What is the function of the final paragraph? How would omitting it have affected the essay?

TONE IN ESSAYS OF OPINION

Tone — the writer's attitude toward his subject — is usually obvious in an essay of opinion. The subject of this essay is the way Americans fill their leisure time — a subject that could have been treated formally and seriously, perhaps even indignantly. But in this essay the author's tone is informal and humorous. *Informality* is evident in the use of short, direct sentences and of phrases like the following:

> A big thing to do with leisure time (lines 5–6)
> All well and good (line 6)
> First off (line 29)

Much of the *humor* results from exaggerating the difficulties involved in the four activities being described:

> Admit that you want to put worms on a hook and angle for sunfish and they will rise from their spinners, flies, and four-ply nylon coelacanth casting line and laugh you out of existence. (lines 31–35)
>
> Modern fishing is as complicated as flying a B-58 to Tacoma. Several years of preliminary library and desk work are essential just to be able to buy equipment without humiliation. (lines 36–39)
>
> It [a sound system] comes in thousands of small electronic parts which must be assembled according to directions in Assyrian. (lines 56–59)
>
> After ruining his first system, the music culturist usually sees the wisdom of a four-year course at the Massachusetts Institute of Technology. (lines 66–68)

What does the exaggeration in each of those sentences indicate about the writer's attitude? Does it suggest that he finds the complications he mentions somewhat absurd? Does he view the amateur pursuit of those leisure-time activities as at least faintly ridiculous?

The author uses technical terms employed in the various activities: "mashie" and "niblick," "tacking" and "keelhauling," "woofer" and "tweeter." How does his use of those terms support his opinion of the various activities? Why do you think he included the terms? In some instances he has misused them. Find out what "keelhauling" (line 45) and "spinnaker" (line 63) mean. Both words are here used incorrectly. Why, do you think? Because the author knows no better, or for some other reason?

Now You Try It

Below are statements of opinion that can be supported and developed by means of examples. Choose one of them, or make up a statement of your own, then support it in a composition containing two or three relevant examples and a concluding paragraph of summary. You may treat your topic either informally and humorously or in a serious, formal manner.

    a. Athletics require more brain than brawn.
    b. What we need today are more good old-fashioned heroes.
    c. The tongue is mightier than the fist.
    d. Advertisements are an education in themselves.
    e. I believe in spending money.
    f. Mongrels make the best pets.
    g. Unhappy experiences are often valuable.

LESSON **23**

Persuasion

Often a writer goes beyond merely expressing an opinion and tries to persuade the reader to pursue a course of action based on it. The models in this lesson exemplify such persuasive writing.

**51   Robert L. Heilbroner in "Don't Let
        Stereotypes Warp Your Judgment"**

[1] Are criminals more likely to be dark than blond? Can a person's nationality be guessed from his photograph? Does the fact that a person wears horn-rimmed glasses imply that he is intelligent?

[2] The answer to each of these questions is, ob-   5
viously, "No."

[3] Yet, from the evidence, many of us believe these and other equally absurd generalizations. Aren't all Latins excitable, all Swedes stolid, all Irish hot-tempered? Think about any group of people — 10
mothers-in-law, teen-agers, truck drivers, bankers — and a standardized picture forms in our heads.

[4] These stereotypes, by which we commonly picture professions, nationalities, races, religions, are closely related to the dark world of prejudice — which means prejudgment. We *prejudge* people, before we ever lay eyes on them.

[5] This irrational stereotyping begins early in life. The child, watching a TV Western, learns to spot the Good Guys and the Bad Guys. Some years ago a psychologist showed how powerful these childhood stereotypes are. He secretly asked the most popular youngsters in an elementary school to make errors in their morning gym exercises. Afterward he asked the class if anyone had noticed any mistakes during gym period. Oh, yes, said the children. But it was the unpopular members of the class — the Bad Guys — they remembered as being out of step.

[6] Stereotypes save us mental effort: they classify into a convenient handful of types the infinite variety of human beings whom we encounter. Thus we avoid the trouble of starting from scratch with each and every human contact in order to find out what our fellow men are really like.

[7] The danger, of course, is that stereotyping may become a substitute for observation. If we form a preconception of all teen-agers as "wild," for example, it doesn't alter our point of view to meet a serious-minded high school student. This is "the exception that proves the rule," we say.

[8] Moreover, quite aside from the injustice it does to others, stereotyping impoverishes us, too. A person who lumps his fellow men into simple categories, who typecasts all labor leaders as "racketeers," all businessmen as "reactionaries," all Harvard men as "snobs," is in danger of becoming a stereotype himself. He loses his capacity to be himself, to see the world in his own unique and independent fashion.

[9] Instead, he votes for the man who fits his standardized picture of what a candidate "should" look like or sound like, buys the goods that someone

in his "situation" in life "should" own, lives the life that others define for him. The mark of the stereo- 55 type person is that he never surprises us, that we do indeed have him "typed." And no one fits this strait-jacket so perfectly as someone whose opinions about others are fixed and inflexible.

[10] Stereotypes are not easy to get rid of. Sharp 60 swings of ideas about people often just substitute one stereotype for another. The true process of change is a slow one that adds bits and pieces of reality to the pictures in our heads until gradually they take on some of the blurredness of life itself. 65

[11] Can we speed the process along? Of course we can.

[12] First, we can become aware of the standard-ized pictures in our heads, in other people's heads, in the world around us. Second, we can be suspi- 70 cious of all judgments that we allow exceptions to "prove." (There is no more chastening thought than that, in the vast intellectual adventure of science, it takes but one tiny exception to topple a whole edi-fice of ideas.) Third, we can learn to be chary * of 75 all generalizations about people.

[13] Most of the time, when we typecast the world, we are not in fact generalizing about people at all. We are only revealing the embarrassing facts about the pictures that hang in the gallery of stereo- 80 types in our own heads.

* **chary:** cautious.

The Writer's Craft

1. What does the essay undertake to persuade the reader to do? Where is the persuasive purpose stated?

2. Do the author's first four paragraphs put the problem of stereotyping before the reader in an interesting way? What is the effect of the questions asked in the first paragraph? Of the examples of stereotypes in paragraph 3? Of the linking of stereo-types to prejudice in paragraph 4?

3. The body of a persuasive essay includes information and statements of personal belief aimed at persuading the reader to accept the writer's opinion and take action on the basis of it. The incident related in paragraph 5 serves the purpose of showing the injustice of stereotyping. In what way?

4. The selection does more than simply appeal to the reader's sense of justice. Paragraphs 7–9 point out the dangers of being a person who forms stereotypes and lives in terms of them. What are those dangers? Does mention of them help convince you that stereotyping is a bad practice for all concerned?

5. In most effective persuasive essays the writer specifies what he wants the reader to do. Where is a way to get rid of stereotypes suggested here? What does the essay suggest the reader should do to help the process along?

6. Is paragraph 13 an effective conclusion for the essay? Why, or why not?

7. Notice that the author uses the first-person plural pronoun (*we, us, our*) throughout the essay; for example:

> These stereotypes by which *we* commonly picture professions, nationalities, races, religions, are closely related to the dark world of prejudice — which means prejudgment. *We* prejudge people before *we* ever lay eyes on them.

By using *we,* he includes himself as one of the offenders. Is that an effective persuasive technique? Explain.

COHERENCE

As in all writing, much of the success of a persuasive essay depends on the writer's ability to make clear the relationships between the various parts that compose it. Those relationships must of course first exist among the ideas themselves, but assuming they do, transitional expressions and linking devices can then help the reader see how each new paragraph grows logically out of the preceding one. How has the author linked the paragraphs in this selection? Are there any places where you feel he should have made the relationship between ideas or paragraphs clearer? If so, explain how you would do it.

WORD CHOICE: CONVEYING AN ATTITUDE

Though the author never directly states his opinion of stereotyping, his attitude is made evident through his choice of words.

How do the italicized words in the following extracts from the model help convey an attitude toward stereotyping?

> . . . many of us believe these and other equally *absurd* generalizations. (lines 7–8)
> This *irrational* stereotyping begins early in life. (lines 18–19)
> The *danger*, of course, is that stereotyping may become a substitute for observation. (lines 36–37)
> Moreover, quite aside from the *injustice* it does to others, stereotyping *impoverishes* us, too. (lines 42–43)
> We are only revealing the *embarrassing* facts about the pictures that hang in the gallery of stereotypes in our own heads. (lines 79–81)

The following essay seeks to persuade us to take an active part in preserving the beauty of the American landscape.

52   Robert H. Boyle in "America Down the Drain?"

[1] This may be the era and the generation and perhaps even the very year that the United States of America, in all its natural glory, goes down the drain. The more I see, the more I am forced to conclude that from New York to California, from Florida to Alaska, America the beautiful is becoming America the ugly, the home of the neon sign, the superduper highway, the billboard, the monotonous housing tract.

[2] Practically all the carnage * is conducted in the name of some kind of alleged ° progress. If this were true progress, no one could have cause for complaint. But, in fact, "progress" has come to stand for stupidity, greed, and graft. We have imperiled the charms of our cities; now the countryside is to be laid waste. The culprits are everywhere: highway builders, conscienceless real-estate dealers, contractors, governments, the Bu-

* **carnage:** destruction.
° **alleged:** so-called.

reau of Reclamation, the Army Corps of Engineers, gutless politicians, power interests (public and private), and industry.

[3] In many ways it is strange that the dismemberment continues, for significant numbers of Americans are concerned about it. Their concern is expressed by architect Edward Durrell Stone, who recently said, "If you look around you, it makes you want to commit suicide." It is expressed by the public interest in such books as Peter Blake's *God's Own Junkyard,* the late Rachel Carson's *Silent Spring,* and Secretary of Interior Stewart Udall's *The Quiet Crisis.*

[4] This concern over the desecration of the landscape is also expressed by angry amateur nature lovers, such as the New Mexicans who defaced billboards on the highway from Santa Fe to Los Alamos. An unknown Canadian, who calls himself the Poetic Carpenter, has gone the New Mexicans one better. Last summer he cut down five billboards along a scenic highway near Kelowna, B.C., leaving behind each time a copy of Ogden Nash's poem:

> I think that I shall never see
> A billboard lovely as a tree.
> Perhaps, unless the billboards fall,
> I'll never see a tree at all.*

[5] The concern displays itself in countless emergency groups that have been organized all over the country to meet specific threats — a highway, a dam, a "sanitary landfill" of a life-giving marsh. All too often, however, their efforts are too little and too late — and even where the effort is strong, it still has little effect. Somehow, representative government seems to have broken down. In instance after instance, politicians, government bureaus, and courts ignore the demands of citizens while they grant a curious immunity to money-grabbers and polluters even when the grossest violation of precedent is involved.

* © 1932 by Ogden Nash, renewed 1960.

[6] Last year, for instance, the National Parks Association, a private group, went to court to try to stop the flooding of Rainbow Bridge National Monument in Utah. The association carried the fight to a U.S. District Court, which dismissed the case on the ground that the association was acting on the behalf of only "the general public."

[7] Another example of the breakdown of representative government concerns the scheduled destruction of an eighteen-mile stretch of the Beaverkill River and its tributary, Willowemoc Creek, in the Catskills, for a four-lane superhighway. These are two of the most famous trout streams in the country, but the New York State Department of Public Works has declared that it not only will run the highway along the banks of the streams but will crisscross them twelve times with concrete bridges. Several thousand residents of the area, many of whom are dependent upon tourists for their livelihood, signed a petition requesting that the highway be built on a natural bench higher up in the valley, thus sparing the streams. The petition resulted in a promise of further study — and, meanwhile, construction has begun on the state's plans.

[8] The following paragraphs give a sampling of just a few more glories that are doomed.

[9] Much of what is left of an original twenty-five-mile strip of the unique Indiana Dunes country on the south shore of Lake Michigan will be torn asunder by steel mills unless Congress passes a bill making it a National Lakeshore. This will turn the area, now a haven for city-weary Chicagoans, into grimy towns like Gary, Hammond, and Whiting.

[10] The Potomac River Basin, a remarkable refuge not only for wildlife but for people, is — if the Army Corps of Engineers has its way — to be dammed and dammed a total of sixteen times to build what is called a chain of "deep-drawdown reservoirs" supposedly needed to maintain the Washington, D.C., water supply, control floods, and abate pollution. "Deep-drawdown" is the bureaucratic way of saying mudhole. The mudholes will scar 70,000 acres of land and cost 400

million dollars, but then the Corps, which is the working arm of the Congressional pork barrel,* has long specialized in superboondoggles.°

[11] The Delaware shore of Delaware Bay, one of the greatest wildlife grounds in the East and home of a seven-million-dollar-a-year fish and oyster industry, is endangered by the proposed construction of a Shell Oil refinery at isolated Blackbird Hundred. The proposed construction site is two miles from Bombay Hook, a refuge on which the federal government has already spent over half a million dollars.

[12] Tierra Verde, a group of Florida islands, borders one of the last great marine nursery grounds of the South. Tierra Verde City, Inc., has already begun to develop 1,120 acres of the nursery grounds, and it plans to dredge up 9,250,000 yards of lush bay bottom that is the basis of a rich marine-life chain. Of course, destruction of the bay would be typical of Florida development. Countless fishing grounds already have been wrecked, including once-fabulous Boca Ciega Bay near St. Petersburg, which has been reduced to a canal system flanked by waterfront homes.

[13] The Hudson Highlands, the magnificent stretch of hills flanking the Hudson River in the vicinity of West Point, are about to become ensnared and befouled by power stations and transmission lines. The Federal Power Commission, which is not in the least concerned with conservation, is expected to give its approval to a proposal by Consolidated Edison for a hydroelectric plant at the foot of Storm King Mountain. Central Hudson Co. has long-range plans for development on the east bank. The Hudson Highlands are within easy driving distance of the eight million beleaguered residents of the smoke, dirt, and noise that is New York City, but this apparently counts for naught.

[14] And so it goes all across the United States, adding to what one British magazine called "the mess that is man-made America." The Bureau of Reclamation,

* **pork barrel:** Federal funds for local projects.
° **superboondoggles:** wasteful, unnecessary projects.

for instance, seriously wants to flood the full length of the Grand Canyon National Monument and up to thirteen miles of Grand Canyon National Park. Grand Canyon, so the Bureau believes, will make a wonderful reservoir.

[15] Other wrecklamation plans are even more improbable. There is a thing known as the Texas Basins Project. It calls for federal funds to be used to divert, by the year 2010, surplus waters in eastern Texas into the Gulf of Mexico, channeling the water into a super-canal ringing the coast. The project would drastically affect one million acres of tidewater that annually yield an average of more than 186 million pounds of commercial fish, shrimp, and oysters and support nearly six million man-days of sport fishing a year.

[16] Apart from the obvious aesthetic * and ethical considerations, there are other valid reasons why this carnage should cease.

[17] For one, there is a desperate need for recreation land, not only as playgrounds for father and son or for fishermen and bird watchers or hikers, but as ties to the biological reality of the world, to the essence of life itself. In many sections of the country too many Americans are becoming alienated from the reality that only parks, natural areas, wild rivers, open spaces, and unblighted seashore can give.

[18] There are economic reasons for saving land. Unspoiled land is money in the bank. Contrary to popular opinion, which equates progress with unmanaged growth, housing developments invariably cost municipalities more money than they produce in taxes. For example, in Cortlandt, a community in northwestern Westchester County, New York, a typical new house pays, on the average, $500 a year in taxes, yet the community has to spend an additional $1500 for services and school costs. In Westport, Conn., the situation has reached the point where any new house costing less than $40,000 will probably be a tax drag on the community.

* **aesthetic:** pertaining to beauty.

[19] There are also scientific reasons for preserving many parts of our landscape. Richard H. Pough, one of the country's leading naturalists and the former chairman of the department of conservation and general ecology * at the American Museum of Natural History, is actively at work attempting to save certain ecologically valuable areas. "As a scientist," Pough says, "I am concerned with the fact that here in North America nature has spent two billion years evolving widely varying plant-animal communities, whose members are uniquely adapted to the soil and climate they occupy. These communities are the living laboratories of the biologist. However, the species are meaningful to the biologist only in terms of the roles they play in the undisturbed community."

[20] Although the situation appears bleak, there are practical steps that can be taken to help offset some of the wreckage. To begin with the most practical step, all conservation interests in the country must join on a national level, no matter how contradictory their aims appear. The Audubon Society must work with Ducks Unlimited and Remington Arms; trout fishermen have to talk to water skiers. Too often, conservationists and sportsmen must realize that their basic aims are the same. If they were united, each interest could retain its own independence and identity, but with one press of a button, all their members could be mobilized into one gigantic army that could fight a specific threat with intelligence and purpose. Then, when the politicians began to count votes, they would have a force to reckon with.

[21] The conservation operations of the federal and state governments need a thorough overhauling. As of now, the federal government has more than thirty bureaus, agencies, and subagencies concerned with conservation. Much of the time they are working at cross-purposes. This waste and duplication of effort is mirrored on state levels. Obviously, these agencies should

* **ecology:** study of the relationship between organisms and their environment.

be brought as much as possible under a coordinating head who would, one assumes, decide on a policy that made sense.

[22] Where state or local governments are uncooperative — and this is the case most of the time — the only thing for angry citizens to do is to band together to form their own pressure bloc. A model group is the Cortlandt Conservation Association in Westchester, New York, which has been functioning for a year. Under the leadership of a no-nonsense president, Mrs. Adolph Elwyn, a science teacher, the CCA has grown from thirty members to four hundred. Considering what had gone on before, wonders have been accomplished. The CCA stopped the dumping of automobiles in a Hudson River marshland; it bought for only $1.25 a fine piece of ravine that came up for auction at a delinquent tax sale; and it is busy piecing together land to ensure that the Croton River gorge will remain forever wild. Any number of experts — ranging from a tree surgeon to a curator at the New York Botanical Garden — serve as consultants to the CCA, and the local politicians and the weekly newspapers are beginning to pay heed.

[23] As Mrs. Elwyn says, "There is no use just sitting by and mourning and allowing the ruin of our country, our waters, and our heritage. We have to get out and do something to stop it. If we try, we may even succeed."

The Writer's Craft

1. The essay begins with the statement of an opinion about what is happening to the American landscape: "America the beautiful is becoming America the ugly." Why is that alarming statement an effective means of beginning the essay?

2. The second paragraph elaborates on the opinion. What is the author's opinion of what has been done to the landscape in the name of "progress"? Whom does he blame? Why do you suppose he lists all the "culprits"?

3. Paragraph 3 begins by pointing out that many Americans are concerned about the destruction of the landscape. Then the

rest of that paragraph and paragraphs 4–7 cite examples of individual and group efforts to stop wasteful and destructive projects. In addition, they tell us that most of those efforts have been unsuccessful — either because they were weak or because the government ignored them. How do paragraphs 3–7 help persuade the reader? In answering, consider both the mention of specific efforts at conservation and the failure of those efforts.

4. Paragraphs 9–15 present details of several destructive projects planned for the future (the article originally appeared late in 1964). Why do you think so many projects are mentioned? Would two or three examples have worked as well? Why do you think projects are cited that are located in various parts of the United States?

5. Paragraphs 16–19 suggest reasons why the landscape should be preserved. What are those reasons? Are they explained in enough detail to be convincing? Do the reasons given here, together with the material in previous paragraphs, persuade you that action to preserve the landscape should be taken? Why, or why not?

6. Paragraphs 20–22 offer three possible ways to stop the present pattern of destruction. What are they? Which course of action is the individual reader most likely to follow? Why do you think the activities of the Cortlandt Conservation Association are described in such detail?

7. Explain why paragraph 23 is a good concluding paragraph for the essay.

Now You Try It

Write an essay in which you express an opinion and try to persuade your reader to follow a particular course of action based on it. Give reasons for holding the opinion, and specify what you would like to see done about the situation to which it refers. You may, if you wish, base your composition on an opinion you have about one of the following subjects:

a. School rules	f. The voting age
b. Required courses	g. The driving age
c. Grades	h. Gossip
d. Homework	i. Violence
e. Tests	j. Welfare

Sentence Skills

THE COMPOUND–COMPLEX SENTENCE

48 David Klein in "Canoes" (page 151)

Earlier you examined the compound sentence and the complex sentence (pp. 108–12). The former coordinates two ideas, whereas the latter subordinates one idea to another to show the relationship between them. The compound-complex sentence, yet another type, combines (as its name suggests) the qualities of both compound and complex sentences. That is, it contains at least two independent clauses and at least one subordinate clause. In the following compound-complex sentences from "Canoes," the subordinate clauses are italicized.

> In recent years the canoe has lost popularity to the more fashionable outboard motorboat and sailboat; but, *if you are willing to make your own decisions instead of following the crowd,* you may well find *that the canoe is not only "the most boat for the money" but also the perfect boat for you.*
>
> Properly cared for, it can last thirty years or more, and *if you get tired of it,* you can sell it for a fairly large fraction of its original cost.
>
> *Because it draws only three to six inches fully loaded,* you can use it in anything larger than a respectable rain puddle, and you can take it into marshes and down shoal rivers *that are unnavigable by any other craft.*

Examine a rewritten version of the third sentence above that expresses the same ideas in a series of simple sentences.

> It draws only three to six inches fully loaded. You can use it in anything larger than a respectable rain puddle. You can take it into marshes and down shoal rivers. Marshes and shoal rivers are unnavigable by any other craft.

Is the writing choppier in this version than it was in the original? Does the series of simple sentences make the relationships between the various ideas clear? Reread the original sentence to see how the relationships are established.

■ **EXERCISE** In the following groups of short sentences strengthen the relationship between the ideas and improve the quality of sentences by rewriting each group as a compound-complex sentence.

1. We emerged into the streets again. The crowds were still heavy. The police were trying unsuccessfully to keep the people in line.
2. The cookies were not as good as Betty had hoped they would be. She did not want to serve them to her friends. They were very critical.
3. The boat was old. The crew and weather were good. We won the race.
4. He was afraid of public speaking. He thought he ought to enter the debate. Debating might be a way to gain respect in the eyes of his fellow students.
5. The researchers gave the monkey a very difficult problem to solve. He could not find a solution. He puzzled over it and worked on it for hours.

GERUND PHRASES

50 Russell Baker in "The Paradox of the New Leisure" (page 159)

Gerund phrases, which work as nouns in sentences, consist of a gerund together with its complements and modifiers. In the following example from "The Paradox of the New Leisure" gerund phrases are italicized:

> In the first place, it means *buying a boat,* then *finding some place to keep the thing,* then *finding someone to explain the difference between tacking and keelhauling*.

Without using gerund phrases, the same ideas might have been expressed by means of a subordinate noun clause:

> In the first place, it means that you buy a boat, then you find some place to keep the thing, then you find someone to explain the difference between tacking and keelhauling.

Gerund phrases are not necessarily preferable to subordinate clauses. There are times, of course, when a subordinate clause must be used to make the relationship between ideas clear. It is helpful, however, to know that gerund phrases are one method by which you can make your writing more concise.

■ **EXERCISE** By following the directions in parentheses, rewrite these sentences so that each contains a gerund phrase. Make any necessary changes in the wording of the sentences.

Example: *If you find the wallet,* you will be rewarded. (Change the italicized adverb clause into a gerund phrase to be used as the subject of the sentence.)

Rewritten: Finding the wallet will bring you a reward.

1. A good furniture finish requires *that you sand the piece until it is as smooth as satin.* (Change the italicized noun clause into a gerund phrase to be used as the object of the verb *requires.*)
2. *If you arrive on time,* you insure a pleasant reception. (Change the italicized adverb clause into a gerund phrase to be used as the subject of the sentence.)
3. *When you plan for an extensive trip,* it takes many hours. (Change the italicized adverb clause to a gerund phrase to be used as the subject of the sentence.)
4. Failure means *that you take the test again at a later date.* (Change the italicized noun clause into a gerund phrase to be used as the object of the verb *means.*)
5. *When you add an extension to an old house,* it sometimes costs more than building an entirely new structure. (Change the italicized adverb phrase into a gerund phrase to be used as the subject of the sentence.)

APPOSITIVES

52   Robert H. Boyle in "America Down the Drain?"
(page 168)

Several sentences in "America Down the Drain?" make use of an appositive (a noun or a pronoun, often with modifiers, set beside another noun or pronoun for the purpose of explaining or identifying it). In the following examples from the selection, appositives are italicized.

> Tierra Verde, *a group of Florida islands,* borders one of the last great marine nursery grounds of the South.
>
> The Delaware shore of Delaware Bay, *one of the greatest wildlife grounds in the East and home of a seven-million-dollar-a-year fish and oyster industry,* is endangered by the proposed construction . . .
>
> This will turn the area, *now a haven for city-weary Chicagoans,* into grimy towns like Gary . . .

On the basis of the sentences above, answer the following questions:

1. What is the usual punctuation for an appositive?
2. Could you remove the appositive and still have complete sentences? Could the appositives stand alone?

Because they save words appositives tighten up writing. For instance, if an appositive had not been used in the first sentence it might have read:

> Tierra Verde, which is a group of Florida islands, borders one of the last great marine nursery grounds of the South.
>
> or
>
> Tierra Verde borders one of the last great marine nursery grounds of the South. Tierra Verde is a group of Florida islands.

Why is the original version better than either of the re-written ones?

■ **EXERCISE** Combine the following pairs of sentences into a single sentence by using appositives.

1. George Murdock is one of the lifeguards at the pool. He is an excellent swimmer.
2. New York City is the largest city in America. It contains many small but distinct neighborhoods.
3. The Wright brothers revolutionized man's concept of space. They were the first men to fly an airplane successfully.
4. Jousting was a favorite sport in the 1500's. It is a contest between two men on horseback and in full armor.
5. Mount Vernon was the home of George Washington. It is a national shrine overlooking the Potomac River.

SECTION SIX

Special Forms

LESSON **24**

The Biographical Sketch

Techniques of description, narration, and exposition apply to virtually all the types of compositions you are called upon to write in school. This section contains a few of those types — a biographical sketch, a character sketch, a personal narrative, and two informal essays — to show how each makes use of what you have already studied. The first model is an example of a biographical sketch, which as you know is a brief narrative presenting the major events and achievements in a person's life.

53 Claude G. Bowers
in "Washington Irving: A National Asset"

[1] A truly observant and constant visitor to the piers of early nineteenth-century New York might well have noticed a young man of slender build who spent most of the day gazing out to sea. His gray-blue eyes were lost in reverie as he dreamed of far places. The dreamer was Washington Irving, who lived near the river front with his father, an unimaginative, austere man. Irving's schooling was rudimentary, for, sad to relate, he was a rather lazy youth. Then, too, his father's financial status was such (he was a successful merchant) as to promise security for a long time to come. In time Irving was admitted to the bar, more as a favor to his family than as a right he had earned.

"I think the young man knows a little law," one bar examiner observed dryly. "Make it stronger," said another. "I would say darn little." Washington Irving never practiced law. He did appear at Aaron Burr's trial for treason with a retainer in his pocket from the defendant, but he was a silent spectator as the really great lawyers crossed swords in verbal combat. It had been the desperate hope of the clever Burr that young Irving's pen might help to acquit him at the bar of public opinion.

[2] In his twenty-first year Washington Irving sailed for a two-year tour of Europe. He visited old churches and art galleries, but he was mostly interested in people. He haunted the theaters, danced, and flirted whenever he found a pretty face. In the diary of his Roman sojourn he wrote that he had visited the churches, but added "to see the faces of the ladies." In Paris he played the dandy, and his diary teems with references to shirtmakers, bootmakers, and tailors. He had money, he was young and gay. The world was indeed his oyster.

[3] Returning to New York, Irving plunged into the social whirl. The unfortunate death of a young girl he loved cast a shadow for a time over his activities. But he recovered sufficiently to woo another, who eventually refused him. Irving was destined to remain unmarried through life, but he never lost his zest for beautiful women.

[4] The gay life he pursued began to drain his resources, and Irving was forced to take up his pen to earn money. With his brother, William, he wrote an amusing book of satirical essays patterned on Addison's *Spectator*. This work, which he called *The Salmagundi Papers*, quickly became the talk of New York. It was followed by *A History of New York*, a humorous work written under the pen name of Diedrich Knickerbocker.

[5] In 1815 Irving returned to Europe for a stay of seventeen years. No American visitor to England, in the days following the troubled years of the War of 1812, did as much to reconcile the two English-

speaking nations as did Irving. During his long stay, his charming personality and manner, his learning and keen intelligence, did much to disabuse the British mind of its dim view of the Americans. In Irving, the English saw an American whom they could admire and respect. Through his eyes they could see an America such as they had not conceived could exist. In them, Irving saw the real English people, and he wrote of what he saw and felt with infinite charm. His understanding and affection glow in his *Sketch Book of Geoffrey Crayon, Gent.*, and in *Bracebridge Hall*. His imagination illuminated for the Americans all he saw. His readers were thrilled, as he was, with the historical scenes, the pageantry of England, the glory he saw.

[6] Irving was welcomed into British literary circles, then at their most glorious. Sir Walter Scott rambled with him in the Scottish hills. The eccentric father of the incredible Disraeli opened to the young American the literary treasures of both his mind and his house. Tom Moore, the Irish poet, was a boon companion and regaled him with his songs. Byron hailed his friendship with delight. He was warmly welcomed to Holland House, where the foremost statesmen and writers of the day gathered.

[7] Back in America the family business failed, and Irving found that he had to write to support himself. He went to Spain and for a time lived with the famous literary collector of the period, Obadiah Rich, in a mansion filled with rare old volumes and priceless manuscripts. It was there that he settled down to write the biography of Christopher Columbus. He went to Seville, to the Archives of the Indies, where he spent days poring over reports of the discoverer's voyages. In time the biography appeared in four volumes.

[8] Irving's research in Seville had intrigued him with the drama of Spain's history, particularly the struggle between the Moors and the Christians. His next book was the stirring history, *The Conquest of Granada*. In Seville Irving lived in an old Moorish palace. Though his apartment was pleasant, the lower floors were let out to tramps and ruffians of the town.

As always, Irving's interest in people was so great that he made friends with his neighbors. From them he heard the strange tales that were to go into his next book, *The Alhambra*. The publication of this book created a lively interest in Spain among other Europeans and Americans, an interest which persists to this day. The late Duke of Alba said that Irving's fascinating book rendered a greater service to Spain than the work of any other writer who followed him.

[9] Returning to New York after his seventeen years in Europe, Irving was hailed enthusiastically, for he had been the first American writer to gain European recognition. The doors of the socially elite were opened to him; writers paid him homage; statesmen acclaimed him as a national asset. Millionaire John Jacob Astor, then eighty, cultivated him. It was during a visit of some days to the Astor mansion that Irving urged the millionaire to devote a part of his fortune to the building of a public library in New York. The talk was to bear fruit when Astor bequeathed money for the purpose, naming Irving as an executor of the will. Thus was started the Astor Library, now The New York Public Library.

[10] It was during the late 1840's that Irving made his tour of the Middle and South West. The result was another book, *A Tour on the Prairies*, filled with many descriptive passages of great beauty. At the request of Astor, Irving wrote *Astoria*, the dramatic story of the fur trade in the far Northwest, where the Astor fortune had been made.

[11] But Europe called him again. Years earlier he had served briefly as secretary of the United States Legation in London. He had found the diplomatic life pleasant. President Tyler, who delighted in his books, offered Irving the post of Minister to Spain. Irving was not particularly fond of politics. He had, in fact, refused the offer of Tammany Hall to make him Mayor of New York. He had also declined President Van Buren's invitation to enter his cabinet as Secretary of the Navy. But a diplomatic post, remote from politics as it was, seemed different.

[12] So, for the next four years, Irving lived in Madrid. In his diaries of the time we see him going through the numerous salons of the Royal Palace to the Porcelain Room to present his credentials to the twelve-year-old Queen, Isabella. With the unscrupulous Queen Mother intriguing to control the throne of Spain, and with the great powers maneuvering to force on the girl a husband of their own choice, Irving's sympathy went out to the little child whom he characterized as "a pawn in a dirty game." He remained the girl's staunch champion throughout his four years as Ambassador. During the civil disturbances and the struggles of various factions for power in Spain, Irving maintained his traditional partiality for the liberals.

[13] But illness began to exact its toll. Irving found himself under doctor's orders neither to read nor to write. His very soul struggled as he spent long hours thinking of his long-projected biography of George Washington. With the election of James Polk as President, Irving resigned and returned home. He bought ten acres on the banks of the Hudson at Tarrytown. There he retired in a house he named "Sunnyside." Now in his seventies, plagued by asthma, weary with the years, Irving shut himself away from the world. Doggedly he wrote on until, a few months before his death in 1859, he finished the fifth and last volume of his biography of our first President.

[14] His course was almost run. Sitting under the trees on the broad lawns of "Sunnyside," his eyes on the Palisades across the Hudson, he passed his last days recalling happy memories. He died in his seventy-sixth year and was buried in the Sleepy Hollow Cemetery. A simple stone marks his resting place.

[15] Washington Irving was the first American writer to gain European acclaim. He gave to the world some of the most delightful and imperishable characters in fiction: Rip Van Winkle, Diedrich Knickerbocker, the Headless Horseman of Sleepy Hollow, and many others who still charm and delight us. His histories and biographies are sound and skillfully written.

Had he produced nothing but his *Sketchbook* and *Tales of the Alhambra* his permanent place in English literature would be assured. No man before him did as much to draw the English-speaking people into a union of fraternity as did he. He was truly an international ambassador of good will.

The Writer's Craft

1. In a biographical sketch, as in most compositions, an effective opening paragraph will usually indicate the subject and arouse the reader's interest in it. How does this sketch of Irving begin? What qualities of Irving do the details in the opening paragraph demonstrate? What background information does the paragraph provide? Do you think more should have been included about Irving's childhood? Why, or why not?

2. The writer of a biographical sketch selects his material carefully to include only highlights — the significant events and achievements — in his subject's life. Often events are presented in chronological order, grouped together in paragraphs that show major periods or phases. The events in this sketch have been grouped chronologically, and according to the places where Irving lived and traveled. Complete the following outline of the major periods and events covered in the sketch:

Paragraph 1: Youth in New York and failure as a lawyer
Paragraph 2: Two-year tour of Europe
Paragraphs 3–4: Return to New York and a gay social life
Paragraphs 5–8: Seventeen years in Europe
Paragraph 9: Return to New York
Paragraph 10:
Paragraphs 11–12:
Paragraphs 13–14:
Paragraph 15:

3. As the model indicates, a biographical sketch covers many events in relatively few words. But in his attempts to be concise, the writer must not overlook the need to show the relationship between events. Sometimes it will be one of cause and effect, as in the first sentence in paragraph 4, where the gay life Irving lived in New York (described in paragraph 3) is identified as the cause of his needing money. That need, in turn, resulted in his writing

The Salmagundi Papers and *A History of New York*. Again, in paragraph 5, Irving's visit to England is shown to have resulted in the publication of two more books. Find at least two other places in the sketch where one event is shown to have caused another.

4. In addition to depicting events in a person's life, a biographical sketch should portray the character and personality of the subject. Where are Irving's personal traits mentioned in this selection? Find at least five places.

5. One way to end a biographical sketch is to describe the last significant event in the subject's life. If the person is dead, the sketch concludes with an account of his death. A different but equally effective concluding paragraph might summarize the subject's achievements. Still another conclusion, if the subject is still living, might project what the person's future activities may be. How does this sketch end? What does the last paragraph accomplish?

Now You Try It

Choose one of the following assignments:

1. Write a biographical sketch, between 350 and 500 words long, of an adult you know well — perhaps a friend or member of your family. To provide material for the composition, interview the person you plan to write about, taking notes on significant events in his life and recording the events and people that have exerted a strong influence on him. Before you begin the composition, arrange the list of events in chronological order, crossing out any you decide not to include. To organize the composition, you may find it helpful to present events according to major periods — childhood, youth, young manhood, and so on. If one event causes another, make the relationship between the two of them clear; and be sure in the course of relating the events to include details that reveal the personality of your subject.

2. Instead of writing about someone else's life, you may, if you wish, write an autobiographical sketch — a brief biography of your own life. Cover only significant events: the birth of a brother or sister, a move to a new neighborhood, meeting a new friend who has influenced you, developing a lasting interest in a school subject or sport or hobby. Plan your autobiography by making a

list of the events you want to include. You may begin with a picture of yourself at present, or with a revealing event from earlier in your life. In the body of the composition, present the major events in chronological order, and in the conclusion look ahead by telling what you plan to do in the future. Since the events you relate will be drawn from your own experiences, you will probably write in the first person, but if you prefer, you may use the third person, as though writing the sketch about someone else. Approximately 350 to 500 words would be an appropriate length for the autobiography.

LESSON **25**

The Character Sketch

Unlike a biographical sketch, which focuses on significant events in a person's life, a character sketch concentrates on revealing personality and character. In other words, it creates a vivid impression of a subject rather than recounting his life story. James Thurber's character sketch, which follows, uses techniques of description, narration, and exposition to let us understand the kind of person his father was.

54   James Thurber in "Gentleman from Indiana"

[1] One day in the summer of 1900, my father was riding a lemon-yellow bicycle that went to pieces in a gleaming and tangled moment, its crossbar falling, the seat sagging, the handlebars buckling, the front wheel hitting a curb and twisting the tire from the rim. He had to carry the wreck home amidst laughter and cries of "Get a horse!" He was a good rider and the first president of the Columbus Bicycle Club, but he was always mightily plagued by the mechanical. He was also plagued by the manufactured, which takes in a great deal more ground. Knobs froze at his touch, doors stuck, lines fouled, the detachable would not detach, the adjustable would not adjust. He could rarely get the top off anything, and he was forever trying to unlock something with the key to something else. In

1908, trying to fix the snap lock of the door to his sons' rabbit pen, he succeeded only after getting inside the cage, where he was imprisoned for three hours with six Belgian hares and thirteen guinea pigs. He had to squat through this ordeal, a posture he elected to endure after attempting to rise and bashing his derby against the chicken wire across the top of the pen.

[2] I am not sure that my father's long, thin face, with its aquiline nose, was right for a derby at any age, but he began wearing one in hard-hat weather when he was only twenty, and he didn't give up the comic, unequal struggle, for the comfort of a felt hat, until the middle nineteen twenties, when he was in his fifties. His daily journeys to the cellar in the winter to stoke the furnace when his three sons were small became a ritual we learned to await with alarm and excitement. He always wore his derby into the cellar, often when he was in bathrobe and slippers, and he always crushed it against one of the furnace pipes. The derby got dented in horse cabs when he climbed in or out, and later against the roofs of automobiles. Since my father was just under six feet, the hat was readily cuffed off by maliciously low doorways and the iron framework of open awnings. At least three times, in my fascinated view, sudden, impish winds at the corner of Broad and High blew the derby off his head and sent it bock-flopping * across the busy and noisy intersection, my father pursuing it slowly, partly crouched, his arms spread out as if he were shooing a flock of mischievous and unpredictable chicks. My mother has fortunately preserved a photograph of him wearing one of his derbies, taken about the time of the Spanish-American War. It shows him sitting on a bench in a park, surrounded by his wife and infant sons, looking haunted and harassed in a derby with an unusually large and blocky crown. In this study he somehow suggests Sherlock Holmes trying to disguise himself as a cabman and being instantly recognized by the far from astute Dr. Watson, rounding a corner and crying,

* **bock-flopping:** a term coined by Thurber to describe the motion of the hat as it was blown across the intersection.

"Great heavens, Holmes, you've muffed it, old fellow! You look precisely like yourself in an enormous bowler."

[3] Everybody's father is a great, good man, someone has said, and mine was no exception. There was never, I truly believe, a purely selfish day in his life. He was sorrowfully aware, from twilight to twilight, that most men, and all children, are continuously caught in one predicament or another, and his shoulder was always ready to help lift a man's cross, or a child's, when it became too heavy to be carried alone. He tried to keep his own plights and griefs to himself, for he hated to bother anybody with his troubles, but everybody wanted him to be happy and everybody did his best to help. When he was secretary to the mayor of Columbus (he often served as unofficial acting mayor) one of his colleagues, in the midst of a political speech, suddenly digressed to talk about my father. "Charley Thurber," he said, remembering some old thoughtfulness, "is the most beloved man in the City Hall." This was conceivably the first time that adjective had ever been publicly used by a municipal employee in any American town.

[4] My father never held a tennis racket or a golf club, and he couldn't kick a football or catch a swift pitch, but he bowled whenever he got a chance — tenpins, duckpins, candlepins, cocked hat, and quintet, a difficult game, the rules for which I was told he had helped to make up. His highest score in tenpins, 269, is the mark of a superior bowler, but he bowled for relaxation and exercise, and not from addiction. He was addicted to contests, contests of any kind. Although he couldn't draw very well, I remember his drawing the Pears' Soap baby, fifty years ago, in a contest for the best pen-and-ink reproduction of the infant in the famous advertisement. He would estimate the number of beans in an enormous jar, write essays, make up slogans, find the hidden figures in trick drawings, write the last line of an unfinished jingle or limerick, praise a product in twenty-five words or fewer, get thousands of words out of a trade name, such as for recent exam-

ple, Planters Peanuts. But it was on proverb contests and book-and-play-title contests, run by newspapers, that he worked hardest. Over a period of fifty years, he won a trip to the St. Louis World's Fair, a diamond ring, a victrola, two hundred dollars' worth of records, and many cash prizes, the largest, fifteen hundred dollars, as first prize in a proverb contest.

[5] Charles L. Thurber was a man of careful method and infinite patience. Once, when the titles of books and plays were printed so close together in a contest catalogue as to be confusing, he cut them out and pasted them on separate strips of cardboard — two thousand separate strips of cardboard. In this way he could compare them, one at a time, with each of the contest drawings, of which there were fifty or more, making at least a hundred thousand permutations in all. He liked to find the less obvious answers: "The Coming of the Tide" for a picture of two youths racing head on and shoulder to shoulder; "Richard the Third" for a drawing of three men on a bench, identified in balloons, from left to right, as Tom, Harry, and Dick. The idiotic answer that paid off on the three men was "Idle Thoughts of an Idle Fellow." Unfair and ridiculous answers are usually picked in every title or proverb contest for five or six key drawings. This is done to prevent experts like Charles L. Thurber from winning all the major prizes in every contest. My father never seemed to get on to this strategy of deceit. He approached every contest with the same light in his eye, confident that the cleverest and subtlest answers would win. His severest disappointment came in 1905, in a proverb contest conducted by the Pittsburgh *Gazette*. I was only ten, but I still remember his anguish over the answer to a drawing showing the figures of a man and a woman in a balloon: "As well out of the world as out of the fashion." The figures were tiny and murky, and he had examined them a hundred times under a hand microscope without detecting that they were dressed any differently from other men and women of the period. In his sixties he gave up his strenuous hobby, reluctantly, but soon decided to in-

vent some contests of his own, to occupy his evening hours. He promptly sold several of them to large newspapers in the Middle West, but when one contest manager suggested that they set up a phony winner and divide the first prize money three ways, he stalked out of the man's office, and his work on contests ended that day. He was easily the most honest man I have ever known.

The Writer's Craft

1. The opening paragraph relates two incidents from the father's experience. One concerns his bicycle; the other involves repairing the children's rabbit pen. What character trait do those incidents illustrate? Where in the paragraph is that trait specifically identified? What is the advantage of beginning the selection with an incident instead of a general statement about the trait?

2. Paragraph 2 describes the father's custom of wearing a derby. Why do you suppose a whole paragraph is devoted to the hat? Does it help convey a sense of what the man who wore it was like? Do details of what happened when he wore the derby add humor to the selection? Paragraph 2 is the only one containing details of the father's appearance; mention is made of his face, nose, and height. Should more details have been included? A complete physical description is rarely provided in a *character* sketch. How does the writer of such a sketch decide which details of his subject's appearance to describe?

3. Paragraph 3 begins with these statements: "Everybody's father is a great, good man, someone has said, and mine was no exception. There was never, I truly believe, a purely selfish day in his life." What facts and incidents are cited to support the statements? The final lines of paragraph 3 quote a remark made about the father. Why are direct quotations about a person effective in a character sketch?

4. Paragraph 4 tells about the father's leisure activities. How did he spend his free time? What does his participation in those activities reveal about his character?

5. The last paragraph includes several incidents that show how much the father loved contests. What character traits do those incidents illustrate? Why do you suppose the author waits

until the end to illustrate and comment on his father's honesty? Hints of that trait appear earlier in the sketch. Where?

6. Because its purpose is to present information about a person, a character sketch is expository. Yet it makes effective use of description and narration as well. By means of specific reference to the model, show how Thurber has used all three kinds of writing here.

Now You Try It

Write a character sketch of someone you know. Avoid telling everything about the person; instead, select two or three outstanding traits to illustrate with incidents and examples. You may find it helpful to follow the pattern of the model by beginning with an incident showing the person performing a typical action. As you relate the incident, or soon afterward, give vital information about the subject — his name, age, and occupation, for instance. Is it important that the reader *see* the person? If so, give details of his physical appearance. After finishing the sketch, reread it to be sure that it creates a vivid impression, making any revisions that you feel will make it more effective.

LESSON **26**
The Personal Narrative

The personal narrative tells, in the first person, a story based on the writer's own experience. Some, such as the one by Sir Edmund Hillary (Model 37), tell of exciting adventures. Others tell about humorous situations and the writer's reactions to them. In the following personal narrative Ruth McKenney tells what happened when she took a lifesaving course at camp.

55 Ruth McKenney in *My Sister Eileen*

[1] From the very beginning of that awful lifesaving course I took the last season I went to girls' camp, I was a marked woman. The rest of the embryo life-savers were little, slender maidens, but I am a peasant type, and I was monstrously big for my fourteen years. I approximated, in poundage anyway, the theoretical adult we energetic young lifesavers were scheduled to rescue, and so I was, for the teacher's purpose, the perfect guinea pig.

[2] The first few days of the course were unpleasant for me, but not terribly dangerous. The elementary lifesaving hold, in case you haven't seen some hapless victim being rescued by our brave beach guardians, is a snakelike arrangement for supporting the drowning citizen with one hand while you paddle him in to shore

with the other. You are supposed to wrap your arm around his neck and shoulders, and keep his head well above water by resting it on your collarbone.

[3] This is all very well in theory, of course, but the trick that none of Miss Folgil's little pupils could master was keeping the victim's nose and mouth above the waterline. Time and again I was held in a viselike grip by one of the earnest students with my whole face an inch or two under the billowing waves.

[4] "No, no, Betsy," Miss Folgil would scream through her megaphone, as I felt the water rush into my lungs. "No, no, you must keep the head a little higher." At this point I would begin to kick and struggle, and generally the pupil would have to let go while I came up for air. Miss Folgil was always very stern with me.

[5] "Ruth," she would shriek from her boat, "I insist! You must allow Betsy to tow you all the way in. We come to Struggling in Lesson Six."

[6] This was but the mere beginning, however. A few lessons later we came to the section of the course where we learned how to undress underwater in forty seconds. Perhaps I should say we came to the point where the *rest* of the pupils learned how to get rid of shoes and such while holding their breaths. I never did.

[7] There was quite a little ceremony connected with this part of the course. Miss Folgil, and some lucky creature named as timekeeper and armed with a stopwatch, rowed the prospective victim out to deep water. The pupil, dressed in high, laced tennis shoes, long stockings, heavy bloomers, and a middy blouse, then stood poised at the end of the boat. When the timekeeper yelled "Go!" the future boon to mankind dived into the water and, while holding her breath under the surface, unlaced her shoes and stripped down to her bathing suit. Miss Folgil never explained what connection, if any, this curious rite had with saving human lives.

[8] I had no middy of my own, so I borrowed one of my sister's. My sister was a slender little thing and I was, as I said, robust, which puts it politely. Eileen

had some trouble wedging me into that middy, and once in it I looked like a stuffed sausage. It never occurred to me how hard it was going to be to get that middy off, especially when it was wet and slippery.

[9] As we rowed out for my ordeal by undressing, Miss Folgil was snappish and bored.

[10] "Hurry up," she said, looking irritated. "Let's get this over with quick. I don't think you're ready to pass the test anyway."

[11] I was good and mad when I jumped off the boat, and determined to make good and show that old Miss Folgil, whom I was beginning to dislike thoroughly. As soon as I was underwater, I got my shoes off, and I had no trouble with the bloomers or stockings. I was just beginning to run out of breath when I held up my arms and started to pull off the middy.

[12] Now, the middy, in the event you don't understand the principle of this girl-child garment, is made with a small head opening, long sleeves, and no front opening. You pull it on and off over your head. You do if you are lucky, that is. I got the middy just past my neck so that my face was covered with heavy linen cloth, when it stuck.

[13] I pulled frantically and my lungs started to burst. Finally I thought the heck with the test, the heck with saving other people's lives, anyway. I came to the surface, a curious sight, my head enfolded in a water-soaked middy blouse. I made a brief sound, a desperate glub-glub, a call for help. My arms were stuck in the middy and I couldn't swim. I went down. I breathed in large quantities of water and linen cloth.

[14] I came up again, making final frantic appeals. Four feet away sat a professional lifesaver, paying absolutely no attention to somebody drowning right under her nose. I went down again, struggling with last panic-stricken feverishness, fighting water and a middy blouse for my life. At this point the timekeeper pointed out to Miss Folgil that I had been under water for eighty-five seconds, which was quite a time for anybody. Miss Folgil was very annoyed, as she hated to get her bathing suit wet, but a thoughtful teacher, she

picked up her megaphone, shouted to the rest of the class on the beach to watch, and dived in after me.

[15] If I say so myself, I gave her quite a time rescuing me. I presented a new and different problem and probably am written up in textbooks now under the heading "What to Do When the Victim Is Entangled in a Tight Middy Blouse." Miss Folgil finally towed my still-breathing body over to the boat, reached for her bowie knife, which she carried on a ring with her whistle, and cut Eileen's middy straight up the front. Then she towed me with Hold No. 2 right in to shore and delivered me up to the class for artificial respiration. I will never forgive the Red Cross for that terrible trip through the water, when I might have been hoisted into the boat and rowed in except for Miss Folgil's overdeveloped sense of drama and pedagogy.

The Writer's Craft

1. This account of what happened to one girl while taking a lifesaving course shows that entertaining narratives can be used on quite ordinary events. In your opinion, what makes the story entertaining? In answering, consider the author's attitude toward herself and the course. Is she complaining about the experience? Is she bitter about it? Does she view it as a series of comic events? How can you tell? Point to specific words and phrases that convey her attitude.

2. Undoubtedly the lifesaving course took several weeks and many lessons to complete, but the narrative tells about only two of the lessons: one on the elementary lifesaving hold and another on undressing underwater. Why do you suppose those two were selected? Why is so much made of the lesson on underwater undressing?

3. The narrative uses description effectively. Find at least three places where descriptive details help you see what is going on. Why do you think the description of a middy occurs in paragraph 12 rather than paragraph 7, where it is first mentioned?

4. As you know, dialogue is an effective means of revealing personality. What does Miss Folgil's speech tell you about her?

5. Writers of personal narratives often exaggerate details and

events to make the story more amusing. For instance, Miss Folgil in real life would hardly have insisted that Ruth stay underwater while Betsy towed her all the way in (paragraphs 4 and 5). Find in the selection at least one other instance of what probably is an exaggeration.

WORD CHOICE: CREATING A HUMOROUS EFFECT

Throughout the narrative the author is smiling at herself and others who participated in the lifesaving course. The humor of the situation is conveyed partly through the author's choice of words. The first paragraph of the selection is reprinted below. Explain how each italicized word or term contributes to the humor of the selection; in doing so, consider other word choices that might have been made.

> From the very beginning of that *awful* livesaving course I took the last season I went to girls' camp, I was a *marked woman*. The rest of the *embryo* lifesavers were little, slender *maidens*, but I am a *peasant type*, and I was *monstrously* big for my fourteen years. I approximated, in poundage anyway, the theoretical adult we energetic young lifesavers were *scheduled* to rescue, and so I was, for the teacher's purpose, the perfect *guinea pig*.

Now You Try It

Write a personal narrative, approximately 350 words long, drawn from your own experience. Present events in chronological order, and make your feelings about them clear. Describe in detail anything you want the reader to see. Some suggested topics are listed below:

a. A different kind of holiday
b. A minor accident or mishap
c. An awkward interview
d. The night the _____ came out (ghosts, alley cats, hives, etc.)
e. My first lesson in _____
f. My first visit to _____ (pick any unusual place)

SPECIAL FORMS

LESSON **27**

The Informal Essay

An informal essay expresses the writer's personal feelings and attitudes toward any phase of life he finds interesting. Appropriate topics — as varied as life itself — range from lighthearted comments on local sports events or current fads to serious reflections on morals or world affairs. To give you an idea of the range of informal essays, two models follow — the first one light, the second one serious.

56   Robert Creamer in "First Pitch"

[1] The American spring is very much like spring anywhere — lively green fingers of things poking their way up through the dull and barren ground, the sudden surprise of tulips, the great, quiet explosion of apple blossoms. 5

[2] These are, in one form or another, universals. But the American spring has something else, too — an element that is rich with the same awakening spirit of rebirth, of life lived again. The boy, sensing the working of the earth, says to his friend: "It 10 smells like baseball." The father picks up the son's

baseball glove and tries it on, working his hand into it, punching it a couple of times.

[3] The gardener rests, letting the sun warm his back, and thinks of the lush summer ahead. The boy and the man think of pitchers and batters, a sharp base hit, an outfielder running, the crowds, the cry of the vendor, the taste of the frankfurter.

[4] The green grass grows, the tulip burns with color, the blossoms gently stroke the air. The ball, the bat, the glove, and the hard (at first), then muddy (for awhile) diamond seem to grow, too, as dormant skills are slowly aroused in the small boy, the young man, the professional.

[5] The sun crosses the equator on its journey north. At that moment, say the precisionists, it is spring. But in America (and perhaps wherever baseball is played) there is another moment. One day a major league pitcher, standing in the center of the formal garden of the infield, working in union with his teammates but isolated from them, takes a deep breath, grasps the slick new baseball, winds up and throws to the opposing batsman. It is the first pitch of the new season.

[6] Then, in America, it is spring.

The Writer's Craft

1. The topic of an informal essay is often an idea or feeling the writer has about some familiar or everyday aspect of life. This essay is based on the close association of spring with baseball in America: the first signs of spring suggest baseball, and the first signs of baseball mean that spring has arrived. In the author's eyes the two events are parallel. What details are included in paragraphs 3, 4, and 5 to show the parallelism? What is mentioned first in each paragraph? What is mentioned second? How do those three paragraphs help reinforce the central idea of the essay?

2. Is the final one-sentence paragraph necessary? How is it linked to the preceding paragraph? How is it related to the entire essay?

3. In enumerating the signs of spring and baseball, the author includes specific descriptions. What words and phrases make the following details vivid?

    a. the sprouts (line 2)
    b. the ground (line 3)
    c. the diamond (lines 21–22)
    d. the infield (line 30)
    e. the baseball (line 32)

WORD CHOICE: FIGURATIVE LANGUAGE

The selection makes effective use of figurative language to describe various aspects of spring. Below are several phrases from "First Pitch" in which examples of figurative language have been italicized. See if you can name the different kinds of figurative language that are illustrated.

> *lively*, green *fingers* of things *poking* their way up (lines 2–3)
> the great, quiet *explosion* of apple blossoms (lines 4–5)
> the tulip *burns* with color, the blossoms gently *stroke* the air (lines 19–20)

Figurative language can help make descriptions fresh and original. Do the examples given above help create a fresh, vivid impression of the familiar happenings of spring? Why, or why not? Why is the phrase "great, quiet explosion" a particularly effective way to describe a flowering apple tree?

> Robert Creamer's informal essay demonstrates how a familiar subject can be treated in an original way. Pearl S. Buck's essay, which follows, shows that an informal essay can discuss matters of serious and lasting importance.

57   Pearl S. Buck in "A Debt to Dickens"

[1] I have long looked for an opportunity to pay a certain debt which I have owed since I was seven years old. Debts are usually burdens, but this is no

ordinary debt, and it is no burden, except as the
feeling of warm gratitude may ache in one until it is ⁵
expressed. My debt is to an Englishman, who long
ago in China rendered an inestimable service to a
small American child. That child was myself and
that Englishman was Charles Dickens. I know no
better way to meet my obligation than to write ¹⁰
down what Charles Dickens did in China for an
American child.

[2] First, you must picture to yourself that child,
living quite solitary in a remote Chinese countryside, in a small mission bungalow perched upon a ¹⁵
hill among the rice fields in the valleys below. In
the near distance wound that deep, treacherous,
golden river, the Yangtse, and some of the most terrifying and sinister, as well as the most delightful
and exciting moments of that child's life were spent ²⁰
beside the river. She loved to crawl along its banks
upon the rocks or upon the muddy flats and watch
for the lifting of the huge four-square nets that
hung into the moving yellow flood, and see out of
that flood come perhaps again and again an empty ²⁵
net, but sometimes great flashing, twisting silver
bodies of fish. She lingered beside villages of boat
folk, and saw them live, the babies tied to a rope
and splashing in the shallower waters. But she saw
babies dead thrown into the deep waters. She wan- ³⁰
dered small and alien among the farm folk in the
earthen houses among the fields. She accepted a
bowl of rice and cabbage often at mealtime and sat
among the peasants on the threshing floor about the
door and ate, usually in silence, listening and lis- ³⁵
tening, answering their kindly, careless questions,
bearing with shy, painful smiles their kind, teasing
laughter at her yellow curls and unfortunate blue
eyes, which they thought so ugly. She was, she
knew, very alien. Upon the streets of the great city ⁴⁰
where sometimes she went she learned to accept the
cry of "foreign devil," and to realize she was a foreign devil. Once when she was very very small, be-

fore she knew better, she turned as worms will, and
flung back a word she had learned among the boat 45
folk when they quarrelled. It was a word so wicked
that the youth who called her foreign devil ran
howling with terror, and thereafter she went more
contentedly, not using the word any more because
of its great wickedness, but knowing she had it to 50
use if she needed it very much.

[3] She grew from a very tiny child into a bigger
child, still knowing she was alien. However kindly
the people about her might be, and they were much
more often kind than not, she knew that she was for- 55
eign to them. And she wondered very much about
her own folk and where they were and how they
looked and at what they played. But she did not
know. In the bungalow were her parents, very busy,
very, very busy, and when she had learned her les- 60
sons in the morning quickly, they were too busy to
pay much heed to her and so she wandered about a
great deal, seeing and learning all sorts of things.
She had fun. But very often she used to wonder,
"Where are the other children like me? What is it 65
like in the country where they live?" She longed
very much, I can remember, to have some of them
to play with. But she never had them.

[4] To this small, isolated creature there came
one day an extraordinary accident. She was an im- 70
possibly voracious * reader. She would like to have
had children's books, but there were none, and so
she read everything — Plutarch's "Lives" and Foxe's
"Martyrs," the Bible, church history, and the hot
spots in Jonathan Edwards' sermons, and conversa- 75
tions out of Shakespeare, and bits of Tennyson and
Browning which she could not understand at all.
Then one day she looked doubtfully at a long row
of somber blue books on a very high shelf. They
were quite beyond her reach. Later she discovered 80
this was because they were novels. But being desperate she put a three-cornered bamboo stool on
top of a small table and climbed up and stared at

* **voracious:** eager, hungry.

the bindings and in faded black titles she read *Oliver Twist*, by Charles Dickens. She was then a little past seven years old. It was a very hot August day, in the afternoon about three o'clock, when the household was asleep, all except the indefatigable parents, and they were very, very busy. She took *Oliver Twist* out of his place — it was fat and thick, for *Hard Times* was bound with it — and in great peril descended, and stopping in the pantry for a pocketful of peanuts, she made off to a secret corner of the veranda into which only a small, agile child could squeeze, and opened the closely printed pages of an old edition, and discovered her playmates.

[5] How can I make you know what that discovery was to that small, lonely child? There in that corner above the country road in China, with vendors passing beneath me, I entered into my own heritage. I cannot tell you about those hours. I know I was roused at six o'clock by the call to my supper, and I looked about dazed, to discover the long rays of the late afternoon sun streaming across the valleys. I remember twice I closed the book and burst into tears, unable to bear the tragedy of Oliver Twist, and then opened it quickly again, burning to know more. I remember, most significant of all, that I forgot to touch a peanut, and my pocket was still quite full when I was called. I went to my supper in a dream, and read as late as I dared in my bed afterward, and slept with the book under my pillow, and woke again in the early morning. When *Oliver Twist* was finished, and after it *Hard Times*, I was wretched with indecision. I felt I must read it all straight over again, and yet I was voracious for that long row of blue books. What was in them? I climbed up again, finally, and put *Oliver Twist* at the beginning, and began on the next one, which was *David Copperfield*. I resolved to read straight through the row and then begin at the beginning once more and read straight through again.

[6] This program I carried on consistently, over

and over, for about ten years, and after that I still [125] kept a Dickens book on hand, so to speak, to dip into and feel myself at home again. Today I have for him a feeling which I have for no other human soul. He opened my eyes to people, he taught me to love all sorts of people, high and low, rich and poor, [130] the old and little children. He taught me to hate hypocrisy and pious mouthing of unctuous * words. He taught me that beneath gruffness there may be kindness, and that kindness is the sweetest thing in the world, and goodness is the best thing in the [135] world. He taught me to despise money grubbing. People today say he is obvious and sentimental and childish in his analysis of character. It may be so, and yet I have found people surprisingly like those he wrote about — the good a little less undiluted, [140] perhaps, and the evil a little more mixed. And I do not regret that simplicity of his, for it had its own virtue. The virtue was a great zest for life. If he saw everything black and white, it was because life rushed out of him strong and clear, full of love and [145] hate. He gave me that zest, that immense joy in life and in people, and in their variety.

[7] He gave me, too, my first real glimpse of a kindly English God, a sort of father, to whom the childlike and the humble might turn. There was no [150] talk of hell in his books. He made Christmas for me a merry, roaring English Christmas, full of goodies and plum puddings and merriment and friendly cheer. I went to his parties over and over again, for I had no others. I remember one dread- [155] ful famine winter the thing that kept me laughing and still a child was *Pickwick Papers*. I read it over and over, and laughed, as I still laugh, over the Wellers and the widow and Mr. Pickwick and all his merry company. They were as real to me as the [160] sad folk outside the compound walls, and they saved me.

[8] And he made me love England. I have no

* **unctuous:** flattering.

drop of English blood in my veins. I have German and Dutch and French ancestors, I was born in the [165] United States of American parents, and I have spent my life in China. But part of me is English, for I love England with a peculiar, possessing love. I do possess something of England. When I went there years later, London was my city and the country- [170] side I knew. I was not strange. The people were my own people too. England is the mother of a certain part of my spirit. I can never take sides against England or the English. It is not only that we speak a common tongue and that we are the same race. [175] There is far more than that. I know English people. I love English people. I have grown up among them. I am used to them. They have been my companions for many years. They are forever my friends. When several years ago in China there was [180] a period of misunderstanding of certain British policies, I steadfastly refused to agree with the distrust expressed by some of my Chinese friends toward England. I was sure of the quality of the English people and of their integrity. What they [185] said they would do, they would do. And they did. Their armies were peacefully withdrawn when the necessity of protection was over. They did not proceed to the conquest the Chinese thought was inevitable, and more than any Western power they [190] have steadily shown their honesty of purpose toward the Chinese. After it was over, my Chinese friends said wondering, "You were right." And I replied, "I knew I was."

[9] This is what Charles Dickens did for me. His [195] influence I cannot lose. He has made himself a part of me forever.

The Writer's Craft

1. What does the first paragraph disclose about the topic of the essay? Does it make you want to know more about Pearl Buck's debt to Dickens?

2. Consider the second sentence in paragraph 1:

> Debts are usually burdens, but this is no ordinary debt, and it is no burden, except as the feeling of warm gratitude may ache in one until it is expressed.

The expression of personal feeling in the sentence is typical of the informal essay. What does the sentence tell you about the writer's character?

3. Paragraphs 2–4, which describe the childhood experiences of an alien in China, are written in the third person; though depicting events from her own life, the writer speaks of herself as "she" and "that child." Why do you think the paragraphs are written in the third person? Does the device help convey a feeling of distance from the experience — as though the writer is remembering something from the far past? Does it help give the paragraphs more of a storylike quality than use of the first person would?

4. Paragraph 5 ends the third-person narration; what follows is in the first person. How is the transition between the two made?

5. There are two parts to the essay: the narrative about the author's childhood, and her explanation of why she is indebted to Dickens. Which paragraph serves as a link between the two parts?

6. Paragraph 6 specifies the first of the many contributions Dickens made to Pearl Buck's life. The list continues through paragraphs 7 and 8. The first of these three paragraphs tells of lasting personal values gained from reading Dickens. Paragraph 7 cites particular kinds of cheer and encouragement received. What influence on her life does the writer discuss in paragraph 8?

7. What is the purpose of the final paragraph?

8. Often an informal essay reveals the writer's feelings and personality. Besides a keen sense of debt and gratitude, what other feelings and values does the author of this essay reveal about herself?

WORD CHOICE: ADJECTIVES

An adjective should, first of all, be necessary; it should not be used to do what a more specific noun could do better. But an adjective that is needed and carefully selected helps make writing exact and vivid. Consider the italicized adjectives in each of the following phrases taken from the model:

> *deep, treacherous golden* river (lines 17–18)
> *moving yellow* flood (line 24)
> *huge, four-square* nets (line 23)
> *great, flashing, twisting, silver* bodies of fish (lines 26–27)
> *shy, painful* smiles (line 37)
> *kind, teasing* laughter (lines 37–38)
> *small, isolated* creature (line 69)

Do the adjectives make the nouns they modify vivid and exact? In any of the phrases could a more specific noun be substituted for the adjective-noun combination? Find at least four other adjectives in the selection, and consider how effectively they have been used.

Now You Try It

Choose one of the following assignments:

1. Write an informal essay showing how a particular person or event influenced your life. The influence may have taken the form of a change in your beliefs, a decision to try something new, or a discovery of a new interest. Make your own choice of what you consider to have been an important influence, then begin with an introductory paragraph that offers some background information on what you were like before you had the significant experience. After you describe the experience, cite examples and incidents to illustrate how it changed you. Conclude by summarizing in a brief paragraph.

2. Choose one of the following general statements to develop in an informal essay, using examples and incidents from your own experience.

   a. Spring brings mud, bugs, and an onslaught of laziness, so why do we long for it so?
   b. A gang can be many things.
   c. Some people have a strange sense of humor.
   d. "We wouldn't worry about what people thought of us if we knew how seldom they did."
   e. Shyness is the price that many people pay for being sensitive.

Sentence Skills

PARTICIPIAL PHRASES

56 **Robert Creamer in "First Pitch"** (page 202)

Participial phrases consist of participles with their complements and modifiers. These phrases function as adjectives, modifying the nouns or pronouns in sentences. In the following sentences from Robert Creamer's essay, the participial phrases are italicized:

> The gardener rests, *letting the sun warm his back,* and thinks of the lush summer ahead.

> One day a major league pitcher, *standing in the center of the formal garden of the infield, working in union with his teammates but isolated from them,* takes a deep breath, grasps the slick new baseball, winds up and throws to the opposing batsman.

As these examples show, the participial phrases are simply another means of conveying information. The same information could, of course, be given in a separate sentence, but that might give it more emphasis than the writer intends. Notice the difference in these two versions of a sentence from Creamer's essay:

Original sentence with information in a participial phrase:

> The boy, *sensing the working of the earth,* says to his friend: "It smells like baseball."

Rewritten so that information is given in a separate sentence:

> *The boy senses the working of the earth.* He says to his friend: "It smells like baseball."

Which version gives more emphasis to the information that the boy sensed the working of the earth? Which version subordinates that information to the idea that the boy said something to his friend?

Generally you will find that participial phrases are an effective way to convey information when you want it to be linked closely with the noun that it explains or describes and at the same time be subordinated to the main idea of the sentence.

■ **EXERCISE** Form a single sentence from each of the following pairs of sentences by changing the sentence in italics into a participial phrase. Place the participial phrase near, or next to, the noun or pronoun it modifies. The rules for punctuating participial phrases are similar to punctuation rules for adjective clauses. Put no commas around participial phrases that are essential to the meaning of the sentence, but do put them before and after phrases that are not essential.

Example: The antique automobiles amused everyone who saw them. *The automobiles chugged and sputtered down Main Street.*

Rewritten: The antique automobiles, chugging and sputtering down Main Street, amused everyone who saw them.

1. The fire soon consumed the entire house. *It sent up great clouds of orange smoke.*
2. The girl staggered down the hall. *She labored under a heavy load of books.*
3. Two dogs woke up the entire neighborhood. *The dogs barked and growled at each other.*
4. Four-year-old Karen screamed with delight at the circus horses. *They pranced and danced around the ring.*
5. A fly kept me awake most of the night. *It buzzed around my head.*

COMPOUND VERBS

57 Pearl S. Buck in "A Debt to Dickens" (page 204)

Wordiness and unnecessary repetition are two pitfalls that a good writer avoids. Using compound verbs (two or more verbs having the same subject) is one way to avoid both. In the following sentences from "A Debt to Dickens," compound verbs are italicized.

But being desperate she *put* a three-cornered bamboo stool on top of a small table and *climbed* up and *stared* at the bindings . . .

I remember twice I *closed* the book and *burst* into tears, unable to bear the tragedy of Oliver Twist, and then *opened* it quickly again, burning to know more.

I *went* to my supper in a dream, and *read* as late as I dared in my bed afterward, and *slept* with the book under my pillow, and *woke* again in the early morning.

▪ EXERCISE Using compound verbs, combine the following groups of sentences into a single, smooth sentence.

1. She walked along the docks. She watched the fishermen lift huge nets filled with fish.
2. He wore a high silk hat. He carried a cane. He always smiled at the neighborhood children.
3. I set the camera on its tripod. I adjusted the lens. I set the time exposure.
4. The tourists climbed into the bus. They gave the driver their tickets. Then they took their seats expectantly.
5. Television introduces us to the performing arts. Television captures news events as they happen. It brings far-off places such as Paris and Tokyo into our living rooms.

SENTENCE SKILLS IN COMBINATION

53 Claude G. Bowers in "Washington Irving: A National Asset" (Page 183)

Many skills are combined in writing good sentences. Though you have examined individual skills in isolation, you should be aware that in any piece of writing all of them work together. The following paragraphs from Bowers' biographical sketch of Washington Irving are illustrative.

The gay life he pursued began to drain his resources, and Irving was forced to take up his pen to earn money. With his brother, William, he wrote an amusing book of satirical essays patterned on Addison's *Spectator*. This work, which he called *The Salmagundi Papers,* quickly became the talk of New

York. It was followed by *A History of New York,* a humorous work written under the pen name of Diedrich Knickerbocker.

In 1815 Irving returned to Europe for a stay of seventeen years. No American visitor to England, in the days following the troubled years of the War of 1812, did as much to reconcile the two English-speaking nations as did Irving. During his long stay, his charming personality and manner, his learning and keen intelligence, did much to disabuse the British mind of its dim view of the Americans. In Irving, the English saw an American whom they could admire and respect. Through his eyes they could see an America such as they had not conceived could exist. In them, Irving saw the real English people, and he wrote of what he saw and felt with infinite charm. His understanding and affection glow in his *Sketch Book of Geoffrey Crayon, Gent.,* and in *Bracebridge Hall.* His imagination illuminated for the Americans all he saw. His readers were thrilled, as he was, with the historical scenes, the pageantry of England, the glory he saw.

Sentences in these paragraphs reflect three basic kinds of sentence variety: *variety in sentence lengths* (from 9 words to 29), *variety in sentence types* (simple, compound, complex, and compound-complex), and *variety in sentence beginnings* (some start with the subject; others, with an adverbial modifier).

Reexamine the two paragraphs and find examples of the following:

1. Two simple sentences
2. Two compound sentences
3. A complex sentence using an adjective clause
4. A complex sentence using a noun clause
5. A complex sentence using an adverb clause
6. One sentence in which an appositive is used
7. Two sentences in which participial phrases are use
8. Three sentences that begin with adverb phrases

■ EXERCISE Rewrite the following paragraphs so that they contain sentences of various types and lengths. Sentences may be combined in several ways. Where ideas in separate sentences are of equal importance, you can coordinate them in compound sentences. Where one idea is clearly subordinate to another, you may put the subordinate idea in a subordinate clause and form a complex sentence; or you may subordinate the idea by turning it into a participial phrase or an appositive. In addition, you may combine sentences that have the same subject by using compound verbs. And you may move modifiers, rearrange the order of sentences, and omit unnecessary words. Begin some sentences with an adverbial modifier and some with the subject.

Barnie burst into his room. He was huffing and puffing. He did not take time to close the door. He picked up his pen. He added the following postscript to a letter he had written to his brother:

"I was walking home from school. A man stopped me. He looked familiar. I couldn't place him. He seemed bewildered. He asked me where Middletown High School was. I told him it was the red-brick building in the next block. He thanked me. He said that he had received directions. He lost them on the train. He wanted to know something. Was the high school auditorium large? I told him it was. He thanked me again. He walked on. I passed a newsstand on the way home. I suddenly realized something. I realized why he looked familiar. The newspaper headline read this way. 'Tex Maloney Will Appear at Benefit Tonight in Middletown High School.' The man I had just talked to was Tex Maloney. Tex Maloney played the hero in the Western you and I saw last Saturday.

Writing About Literature

LESSON **28**
Writing About Fiction

Many compositions you write in school analyze some aspect of literature found in novels, stories, or poems you read. If you read carefully, then apply what you have already learned about composition, you will not find analytical writing difficult. The procedure is relatively straightforward.

Suppose that you are asked to analyze a work of fiction — a short story, for example. First you must read the story, perhaps once and then a second time more carefully. As you read, note the aspects of the story that particularly interest or impress you, for much of the merit of your analysis will depend on your having discovered an interesting insight to analyze. You may choose to write about a theme that the story expresses, or about the characters in it, or about how the plot develops, or about the vividness of the setting, or about the point of view from which the story is told, or about some relevant relationship among those various elements. The possibilities are many, but make sure you select an insight that strikes you as both valid and interesting.

Having settled on the insight, state it as clearly as you can in the form of a general sentence. (Remember that *general* and *vague* are not synonymous.) Then look back through the story to find details that support the insight most effectively. Note those details, for you will use them in developing the composition.

To write the composition itself, you should apply the skills you have studied and used in earlier lessons on expository writing. Unify the analysis by keeping the insight clearly in mind. Is what you are saying related to it? If not, omit that detail. And to give the composition coherence, show *how* the details are related and present them in some logical order. One suggestion: use transitional words and phrases liberally. Most student writers use too few of them; by becoming aware of the variety and usefulness of such expressions (*for example, however, consequently, moreover, next, most important, besides, in addition,* and so on), you will be training yourself to think coherently of the relationships between the various ideas you set down.

The following story provides an opportunity to practice writing about fiction. Read it, then consider the suggestions that follow on how to write about it effectively.

Masculine Protest

FRANK O'CONNOR

For months things had been getting worse between Mother and me. At the time I was twelve, and we were living in Boharna, a small town twenty miles from the city — Father, Mother, Martha, and I. Father worked in the County Council and we 5
didn't see much of him. I suppose that threw me more on Mother, but I could be perfectly happy sitting with her all day if only she let me. She didn't, though. She was always inventing excuses to get rid of me, even giving me money to go to the pictures, 10
which she knew Father didn't like because I wasn't very bright at school and he thought the pictures were bad for me.

I blamed a lot of it on Martha at first. Martha was sly, and she was always trying to get inside me with 15
Mother. She was always saving, whereas I always found money burned a hole in my pocket, and it was only to spite her that I kept a savings bank at all. As well as that, she told Mother about all the scrapes I got into. They weren't what you'd really 20
call scrapes. It was just that we had a gang in our neighborhood which was the classy one of the town, and we were always having battles with the kids from the other side of town who wanted to

play in our neighborhood. I was the Chief Gang ²⁵ Leader, and it was my job to keep them from expanding beyond their own frontiers.

Martha let on not to understand why I should be Chief Gang Leader. She let on not to know why we didn't want the other kids overrunning our locality. ³⁰ Though she knew better than to tell Mother when I made Viking raids on the housekeeping money, she was always at me in a low, blood-curdling voice, following me round like a witch. "You'll be caught, yet, Denis Halligan. You'll be caught. The police ³⁵ will be after you. You took three shillings out of Mummy's purse. God sees you!" Sometimes she drove me so wild that I went mad and twisted her arm or pulled her hair, and she went off screeching, and I got a licking. ⁴⁰

I had managed to kid myself into the belief that one day Mother would understand; one day she would wake up and see that the affection of Dad and Martha was insincere; that the two of them had long ago ganged up against her, and that I, the ⁴⁵ black sheep, was the one who really loved her.

This revelation was due to take place in rather unusual circumstances. We were all to be stranded in some dangerous desert, and Mother, with her ankle broken, would tell us to leave her to her fate, ⁵⁰ the way they did in storybooks. Dad and Martha, of course, would leave her, with only a pretense of concern, but I, in my casual way, would simply fold my hands about my knees and ask listlessly: "What use is life to me without you?" Nothing ⁵⁵ more; I was against any false drama, any raising of the voice. I had never been one for high-flown expressions like Martha: just the lift of the shoulder, the way I pulled a grass-blade to chew (it needn't be a desert), and Mother would realize at last that ⁶⁰ though I wasn't demonstrative — just a plain, rough, willing chap—I really had a heart of gold.

The trouble about Mother was that she had a genius for subjecting hearts of gold to intolerable strain. It wasn't that she was actively unkind, for ⁶⁵

she thought far too much of the impression she wanted to make to be anything like that. It was just that she didn't care. She was always away from home. She visited friends in Galway, Dublin, Birr, and Athlone, and all we ever got to see of her was the flurry between one foray and the next, while she was packing and unpacking.

Things came to a head when she told me she wouldn't be at home for my birthday. At the same time, always conscientious, she had arranged a very nice treat for Martha and me. But the treat wasn't the same thing that I had been planning, when I proposed to bring a couple of fellows along and show Mother off to them, and I began to bawl. The trouble was that the moment I did, I seemed to have no reasons on my side. It was always like that with Mother; she invariably had all the reasons on her side, and made you feel contrary and a pig, but that was worse instead of better. You felt then that she was taking advantage of you. I sobbed and stamped and asked why she hadn't done that to Martha and why she was doing it to me. She looked at me coldly and said I was a pretty picture and that I had no manliness. Of course, I saw she was in the right about that too, and that there was no excuse for a fellow of my age complaining against not being treated like his younger sister, and that only made me madder still.

"Go on!" I screamed. "Who's trying to stop you? All you want is people to admire you."

I knew when I had said it that it was awful, and expected her to give me a clout, but she only drew herself up, looking twice as dignified and beautiful.

"That is a contemptible remark, Denis," she said in a biting tone. "It's one I wouldn't have expected even from you."

The way she said it made me feel like the scum of the earth. And then she went off for the evening in a car with the Clarkes, leaving Martha and me alone. Martha looked at me, half in pity, half in amusement. She was never really disappointed in Mother, because she expected less of her. Martha was born sly.

"What did I tell you?" she said, though she hadn't told me anything. [110]

"Go on!" I said in a thick voice. "You sucker!" Then I went upstairs and bawled and used all the dirty words I knew. I knew now it was all over between Mother and me; that no circumstances would ever occur which would show how much I loved [115] her, because after what had happened I could not live in the same house with her again. For quite a while I thought about suicide, but I put that on one side, because the only way I could contemplate committing suicide was by shooting, and my air [120] pistol was not strong enough for that. I took out my post-office book. I had four pounds fifteen in the bank. As I've said, it was purely out of spite against Martha, but that made no difference now. It was enough to keep me for a month or so till I found [125] some corner where people wanted me: a plain rough-spoken chap who only needed a little affection. I was afraid of nothing in the way of work. I was strong and energetic. At the worst, I could always make for Dublin, where my grandfather and [130] Auntie May lived. I knew they would be glad to help me, because they thought that Dad had married the wrong woman and never pretended to like Mother. When Mother had told me this I was furious, but now I saw that they were probably cleverer [135] than I was. It would give me great satisfaction to reach their door and tell Auntie May in my plain straightforward way: "You were right and I was wrong." For the last time I looked round my bedroom and burst into fresh tears. There is something [140] heart-rending about leaving for the last time a place where you have spent so much of your life. Then, trying to steady myself, I grabbed a little holy picture from the mantlepiece and a favorite storybook from the book shelf and ran downstairs. Martha [145] heard me taking out my bike and came to see. It had a dynamo lamp and a three-speed gear: a smashing bike!

"Where are you off to?" she asked.

"Never mind!" I said as I cycled off. 150

I had no particular feelings about seeing Martha for the last time.

Then I had my first shock, because as I cycled into Main Street I saw that all the shops were shuttered for the weekly half-holiday and I knew the 155 post office would be shut too and I could not draw out my savings. It was the first time I felt what people so often feel in afterlife, that Fate has made a plaything of you. Why should I have had my final quarrel with Mother on the one day in the week 160 when I could not get away from her? If that wasn't Fate, what was? And I knew my own weakness of character better than anyone. I knew that if I put it off until next day, the sight of Mother would be sufficient to set me servilely seeking for pardon. 165 Even setting off across Ireland without a penny would be better than that.

Then I had what I thought was an inspiration. The city was only twenty miles away, and the General Post Office was bound to be open. I had cal- 170 culated my time to and from school at twelve miles an hour; even allowing for the distance, it wouldn't take me more than two hours. As well as that, I had been to the city for the Christmas shopping, so I knew the look of it. I could get my money and stay 175 in a hotel or have tea and then set off for Dublin. I liked that idea. Cycling all the way up through Ireland in the dark, through sleeping towns and villages; seeing the dawn break over Dublin as I cycled down the slopes of the Dublin mountains; 180 arriving at Auntie May's door in the Shelbourne Road when she was lighting the fire — that would be smashing. I could imagine how she would greet me — "Child of grace, where did you come from?" "Ah, just cycled." My natural modesty always came out 185 in those daydreams of mine, for I never, under any circumstances, made a fuss. Absolutely smashing!

All the same, it was no joke, a trip like that. I cycled slowly and undecidedly out the familiar main road where we walked on Sunday, past the [190] little suburban houses. It was queer how hard it was to break away from places and people and things you knew. I thought of letting it go and of doing the best I could to patch it up with Mother. I thought of the gang and at that a real lump rose [195] in my throat. Tomorrow night, when my absence was noticed, there would be a new Chief Gang Leader; somebody like Eddie Humphreys who would be so prim and cautious that he would be afraid to engage the enemy which threatened us on [200] every side. In that moment of weakness I nearly turned back. At the same moment it brought me renewed decision for I knew that I had not been chosen Chief Gang Leader because I was a little sissy like Eddie Humphreys but because I was [205] afraid of nothing.

At one moment my feet had nearly stopped pedaling, at the next I was pedaling for all I was worth. It was as sudden as that, like the moment when you find yourself out of your depth and two inclina- [210] tions struggle in you — to swim back to the shallows or strike out boldly for the other side. Up to that I had thought mainly of what was behind me; now I thought only of what was ahead of me, and it was frightening enough. I was aware of great distances, [215] of big cloud masses on the horizon, of the fragility of my tires compared with the rough surface of the road, and I thought only of the two-hour journey ahead of me. The romantic picture of myself cycling across Ireland in the dark disappeared. I [220] should be quite content to get the first stage over me.

For the last ten miles I wasn't even tempted to look at the scenery. I was doubled over the handlebars. Things just happened; the road bent away under me; wide green rivers rose up and slipped away [225] again under me; castles soared from the roadside with great arches blocked out in masses of shadow.

Then at last the little rocky fields closed behind me like a book, and the blessed electric-light poles escorted me up the last hill, and I floated proudly down between comfortable villas with long gardens till I reached the bridge. The city was stretched out on the other side of the river, shining in the evening light, and my heart rose at the thought that I had at least shown Mother whether or not I had manliness. I dismounted from my bicycle and pushed it along the Main Street, looking at the shops. They were far more interesting than the shops at home, and the people looked better too.

I found the post office in a side street and went up to the counter with my savings-bank book.

"I want to draw out my money," I said.

The clerk looked at the clock.

"You can't do that, sonny," he said. "The savings-bank counter is shut."

"When will it open again?" I asked.

"Not till tomorrow. Any time after nine."

"But can't I get it now?"

"No. The clerk is gone home now."

I slouched out of the post office with despair in my heart. I took my bicycle and pushed it wearily back to the Main Street. The crowds were still going by, but now it looked long and wide and lonesome, for I had no money and I didn't know a soul. Without a meal and a rest, I could not even set out for Dublin, if I had the heart, which I knew I hadn't. Nor could I ever return home, for it was already late and I was dropping with weariness. One side of Main Street was in shadow; the shadow seemed to spread with extraordinary rapidity, and you felt that the city was being quenched as with snuffers.

It was only then that I thought of Father. It was funny that I had not thought of him before, even when thinking of Grandfather and Auntie May. I had thought of these as allies against Mother, but I hadn't even considered him as an ally. Now as I thought of him, everything about him seemed dif-

ferent. It wasn't only the hunger and panic. It was
something new for me. It was almost love. With 270
fresh energy I pushed my bicycle back to the post
office, left it outside the door where I could see it,
and went up to the clerk I had already spoken to.

"Could I make a telephone call?" I asked.

"You could to be sure," he said. "Have you the 275
money?"

"No, sir."

"Well, you can't make a call without the money.
Where is it to?"

"Boharna," I said.   280

At once his face took on a severe expression.

"That's one and threepence," he said.

"And I can't ring unless I have the money?"

"Begor, you can't. I couldn't ring myself without
that."   285

I went out and took my bicycle again. This time I
could see no way out. I dawdled along the street,
leaving my bicycle by the curb and gazing in shop
windows. In one I found a mirror in which I could
see myself full length. I looked old and heart- 290
broken. It was just like a picture of a child without a
home, and I blinked away my tears.

Then, as I approached a public house, I saw a
barman in shirt sleeves standing by the door. I remembered that I had seen him already on my way 295
down and that he had looked at me. He nodded and
smiled and I stopped. I was glad of anyone making a friendly gesture in that strange place.

"Are you waiting for someone?" he asked.

"No," I said. "I wanted to make a phone call."   300

"You're not from these parts?"

"No,"I said. "I'm from Boharna."

"Are you, begor?" he said. "Was it on the bus you
came?"

"No," I replied modestly. "I biked it."   305

"Biked it?"

"Yes."

"That's a distance," he said.

"It is long," I agreed.

"What did you come all that way for?" he asked [310] in surprise.

"Ah, I was running away from home," I said despondently.

"You were what?" he asked in astonishment. "You're not serious." [315]

"But I am," I said, very close to tears. "I did my best, but then I couldn't stick it any longer and I cleared out." I turned my head away because this time I was really crying.

"Oh, begor, I know what 'tis like," he said in a [320] friendlier tone. "I did it myself."

"Did you?" I asked eagerly, forgetting my grief. This, I felt, was the very man I wanted to meet.

"Ah, indeed I did. I did it three times what's more. By that time they were getting fed up with [325] me. Anyway, they say practice makes perfect. Tell me, is it your old fellow?"

"No," I said with a sigh. "My mother."

"Ah, do tell me so? That's worse again. 'Tis bad enough to have the old man at you, but 'tis the devil [330] entirely when the mother is against you. What are you going to do now?"

"I don't know," I said. "I wanted to get to Dublin, but the savings bank is shut, and all my money is in it." [335]

"That's tough luck. Sure, you can't get anywhere without money. I'm afraid you'll have to go back and put up with it for another while."

"But I can't." I said. " 'Tis twenty miles."

" 'Tis all of that, begor. You couldn't go on the [340] bus?"

"I can't. I haven't the money. That's what I asked them in the post office, to let me ring up Daddy, but they wouldn't."

"Where's your daddy?" he asked, and when I [345] told him: "Ah, we'll try and get him for you anyway. Come on in."

There was a phone in the corner, and he rang up and asked for Daddy. Then he gave me a big

smile and handed me the receiver. I heard Daddy's 350
voice and I nearly wept with delight.

"Hullo, son," he said in astonishment. "Where on
earth are you?"

"In the city, Daddy," I said modestly — even then
I couldn't bring myself to make a lot of it, the way 355
another fellow would.

"The city?" he repeated incredulously. "What
took you there?"

"I ran away from home, Dad," I said, trying to
make it sound as casual as possible. 360

"Oh!" he exclaimed and there was a moment's
pause. I was afraid he was going to get angry, but
his tone remained the same. "Had a row?"

"Yes, Dad."

"And how did you get there?" 365

"On the bike."

"All the way? But you must be dead."

"Just a bit tired," I said modestly.

"Tell me, did you even get a meal?"

"No, Dad. The savings bank was shut." 370

"Ah, blazes!" he said softly. "Of course, it's the
half day. And what are you going to do now?"

"I don't know, Dad. I thought you might tell me."

"Well, what about coming home?" he said, beginning to laugh. 375

"I don't mind, Dad. Whatever you say."

"Hold on now till I see what the buses are
like. . . . Hullo! You can get one in forty minutes'
time — seven ten. Tell the conductor I'll be meeting
you and I'll pay your fare. Will that be all right?" 380

"That's grand, Dad," I said, feeling that the world
was almost right again.

When I finished, the barman was waiting for me
with his coat on. He had got another man to look
after the bar for him. 385

"Now, you'd better come and have a cup of tea
with me before your bus goes," he said. "The old
bike will be safe outside."

He took me to a café, and I ate cake after cake

and drank tea and he told me about how he'd run [390] away himself. You could see he was a real hard case, worse even than I was. The first time, he'd pinched a bicycle and cycled all the way to Dublin, sleeping in barns and deserted cottages. The police had brought him home and his father had belted [395] him. They caught him again the second time, but the third time he'd joined the army and not returned home for years.

He put me and my bicycle on the bus and paid my fare. He made me promise to tell Dad that he'd [400] done it and that Dad owed me the money. He said in this world you had to stand up for your rights. He was a rough chap, but you could see he had a good heart. It struck me that maybe only rough chaps had hearts as good as that. [405]

Dad was waiting for me at the bus stop, and he looked at me and laughed.

"Well, the gouger!" he said. "Who ever would think that the son of a good-living, upright man like me would turn into a common tramp." [410]

All the same I could see he was pleased, and as he pushed my bike down the street he made me tell him all about my experiences. He laughed over the barman and promised to give me the fare. Then, seeing him so friendly, I asked the question that [415] had been on my mind the whole way back on the bus.

"Mummy back yet, Dad?"

"No, son," he said. "Not yet. She probably won't be in till late." [420]

What I was really asking him, of course, was "Does she know?" and now I was torn by the desire to ask him not to tell her, but it choked me. It would have seemed too much like trying to gang up against her. But he seemed to know what I was [425] thinking, for he added with a sort of careful casualness that he had sent Martha to the pictures. I guessed that that was to get her out of the way so that she couldn't bring the story to Mother, and

when we had supper together and washed up after- 430
ward, I knew I was right.

Mother came in before we went to bed, and Father talked to her just as though nothing had happened. He was a little bit more forthcoming than
usual, but that was the only indication he gave, and 435
I was fascinated, watching him create an understanding between us. It was an understanding in
more ways than one, because it dawned on me
gradually that, like myself and the barman, Dad too
had once run away from home, and for some rea- 440
son — perhaps because the bank was shut or because he was hungry, tired, and lonely — he had
come back. People mostly came back, but their protest remained to distinguish them from all the others who had never run away. It was the real sign of 445
their manhood.

I never ran away after that. I never felt I needed
to.

Writing About "Masculine Protest"

Suppose, having read the story, you find yourself most interested in Denis, the main character. He might well be the subject
of a composition based on "Masculine Protest." Is he selfish? Is
he childish? Is he believable? What sort of boy is he? One possible statement about Denis is given below, followed by a list of
supporting details from the story.

General Statement:

Denis Halligan, the main character in "Masculine Protest," has
a vivid imagination and a highly developed sense of drama.

Supporting Details:

1. Unhappy with the way his mother treats him, Denis imagines a scene in which she will finally realize his worth. In
   this scene he sees his family stranded in a dangerous
   desert. His mother, who has broken an ankle, is abandoned
   by his sister and father "with only a pretense of concern."
   Denis, as the hero, remains behind to show his love for his

mother, declaring dramatically, "What use is life to me without you?" She then recognizes that he has a "heart of gold." (lines 41–62)

2. Disappointed by his mother's not being home for his birthday celebration, Denis reacts dramatically. He feels that he can no longer live in the same house with her and for a while thinks about suicide. Finally he decides to leave home to find a place where people want him and will give him "a little affection." He thinks of going to Dublin to his grandfather and aunt, who do not like his mother, and imagines his satisfaction in reaching their door and saying: "You were right and I was wrong." (lines 113–39)

3. When he discovers that he must ride to a city twenty miles away to get his money, he imagines that he can still get to Dublin by "cycling all the way up through Ireland in the dark." He sees himself arriving at his aunt's door just as she is lighting the fire. This scene appeals to Denis's love of the dramatic. He even imagines the dialogue that will take place between himself and his aunt when he arrives, and feels that the whole scene will be "absolutely smashing!" (lines 168–87)

4. As Denis proceeds on his twenty-mile ride to the city, his romantic picture of himself disappears, but it reappears when he finally arrives and imagines that he has shown his mother that he is a man. (lines 207–35)

Notice, incidentally, that the statement and supporting details are written in the present tense; you should follow that practice in your own analytical writing. It is conventional — and effective — to use the present tense consistently, indicating past action by means of the present perfect tense: "His mother, who *has broken* her ankle . . ." etc. In that way, what you write will seem much more alive and vital; the past tense, on the other hand, has a way of making your comments on the story seem lifeless, and the story itself as dead as yesterday's newspaper.

But to return to content. Be sure to select relevant details to include; don't simply summarize the story. The details above are listed in the order in which they occur in "Masculine Protest." Other arrangements are possible, however — and often preferable. Most obviously, you might present details according to the order of their importance (page 32). But whatever order you finally decide on, indicate it clearly by means of transitional expressions.

Probably you would be wisest to begin with the general statement about the story. As you proceed, add your own comments on the details included, and provide words and phrases that let the essay flow smoothly forward through all the details to the conclusion. One possible conclusion for the essay outlined above might effectively be composed of a sentence or two explaining how Denis's daydreams influence your impression of him.

Now You Try It

1. Write a brief composition about "Masculine Protest." You may either use one of the following general statements as your topic or choose a topic of your own. At the beginning of the composition, state the topic concisely, then develop it by citing specific details from the story and commenting on them.

a. In "Masculine Protest" Denis Halligan sees a different world from the one his mother sees. (Develop by comparing and contrasting the two views.)

b. Denis Halligan, the chief character in "Masculine Protest," is a recognizable twelve-year-old. (Develop by mentioning and illustrating character traits typical of twelve-year-olds.)

c. Indirectly we learn a lot about Denis Halligan's mother in "Masculine Protest." (Develop by giving evidence of the kind of woman she is.)

d. "Masculine Protest" explores some of the conflicts between the dream world of children and the real world of adults. (Develop by comparing and contrasting the two worlds.)

e. "Masculine Protest" raises the question of what true manliness is. (Develop by comparing the implied definitions of that term as it is used in the story.)

f. "Masculine Protest" is a story about a boy who comes to understand and appreciate his family. (Develop by explaining how he comes to that understanding, and what it is. Avoid simply summarizing the story.)

g. "Masculine Protest" would be an entirely different story told from the father's point of view. (Develop by indicating in what ways the story would be changed.)

h. In "Masculine Protest" a boy who runs away from home finally becomes wiser and more mature. (Develop by comparing Denis's attitudes before leaving with those after his return home.)

2. Write a composition about a short story or novel you have read recently. Early in the composition identify the work and its author, and make a general statement about some aspect of it. Develop the composition with supporting details presented in a logical and effective order. Revise until you have produced a composition that represents your best work.

LESSON **29**

Writing About Poetry

As with fiction, a composition about poetry should be clear, concrete, and effectively organized. Any general statements you make in the course of the composition should be supported with specific details, drawn both from the poem or poems being considered and from your own understanding. In citing details you may either quote verses and phrases directly or, as a variation, paraphrase or briefly summarize the meaning of specific verses. If you paraphrase, be sure the words and style are your own. It is better to quote directly than to paraphrase too closely.

The following pages contain six pairs of poems. Read all of them carefully and more than once, observing how the members of each pair are comparable. Then select one pair to use as the basis for a composition. You may compare or contrast the ideas or feelings expressed in the poems, or you may analyze the two poems to arrive at a preference. In the latter case, don't start by announcing which poem you prefer; it is far more effective to end with the statement of preference, having given your reasons for feeling as you do in the preceding analysis.

Before starting to write, reread both poems attentively, several times if necessary, looking for points of comparison to use as a composition topic. A way to approach the Millay and Masefield poems, for example, might be to consider the attitude toward the city and the sea that the poets express. If you decide that their feelings are similar, you might use that similarity as the basis of the composition, citing details from the poems to support your insight. You might also approach the poems by considering details of the sea included in each, in order to decide which poem creates an impression of the sea more vividly. There are, of course, still other ways to analyze the two poems, and as you examine them, you will undoubtedly develop your own ideas about what you want to say and how best to say it.

Entitle your composition in a way that makes clear which pair of poems you are comparing, and in the composition itself make clear to which poem you are referring when you cite specific details or state an opinion. There are no set limits for the length of this composition. Depending on how much you have to say, it may be as short as a couple of paragraphs or as long as two or three pages.

PAIR I

Exiled

EDNA ST. VINCENT MILLAY

Searching my heart for its true sorrow,
    This is the thing I find to be:
That I am weary of words and people,
    Sick of the city, wanting the sea;

Wanting the sticky, salty sweetness   5
    Of the strong wind and shattered spray;
Wanting the loud sound and the soft sound
    Of the big surf that breaks all day.

Always before about my dooryard,
    Marking the reach of the winter sea,   10
Rooted in sand and dragging driftwood,
    Straggled the purple wild sweetpea;

Always I climbed the wave at morning,
  Shook the sand from my shoes at night,
That now am caught beneath great buildings, 15
  Stricken with noise, confused with light.

If I could hear the green piles groaning
  Under the windy wooden piers,
See once again the bobbing barrels,
  And the black sticks that fence the weirs,° 20

If I could see the weedy mussels
  Crusting the wrecked and rotting hulls,
Hear once again the hungry crying
  Overhead, of the wheeling gulls,

Feel once again the shanty straining 25
  Under the turning of the tide,
Fear once again the rising freshet,°
  Dread the bell in the fog outside, —

I should be happy, — that was happy
  All day long on the coast of Maine! 30
I have a need to hold and handle
  Shells and anchors and ships again!

I should be happy, that am happy
  Never at all since I came here.
I am too long away from water. 35
  I have a need of water near.

20. **weirs:** places in which to catch fish.
27. **freshet:** sudden stream of fresh water.

A Wanderer's Song

JOHN MASEFIELD

A wind's in the heart of me, a fire's in my heels,
I am tired of brick and stone and rumbling wagon wheels;
I hunger for the sea's edge, the limits of the land,
Where the wild old Atlantic is shouting on the sand.

Oh, I'll be going, leaving the noises of the street,   5
To where a lifting foresail foot is yanking at the sheet; °
To a windy, tossing anchorage where yawls and ketches ° ride,
Oh I'll be going, going, until I meet the tide.

And first I'll hear the sea wind, the mewing of the gulls,
The clucking, sucking of the sea about the rusty hulls,   10
The songs at the capstan ° in the hooker ° warping out,°
And then the heart of me'll know I'm there or thereabout.

Oh I am tired of brick and stone, the heart of me is sick,
For windy green, unquiet sea, the realm of Moby Dick;
And I'll be going, going, from the roaring of the wheels,   15
For a wind's in the heart of me, a fire's in my heels.

    6. **sheet:** rope attached to lower end of a sail.
    7. **yawls and ketches:** types of sailboats.
    11. **capstan:** a drumlike apparatus used to hoist anchor and
        other weights; **hooker:** an old ship; **warping out:** being
        pulled out of the harbor.

PAIR II

Leisure

W. H. DAVIES

What is this life if, full of care,
We have no time to stand and stare.

No time to stand beneath the boughs
And stare as long as sheep or cows.

No time to see, when woods we pass,   5
Where squirrels hide their nuts in grass.

No time to see, in broad daylight,
Streams full of stars, like skies at night.

No time to turn at Beauty's glance,
And watch her feet, how they can dance. 10

A poor life this if, full of care,
We have no time to stand and stare.

I Meant to Do My Work Today

RICHARD LE GALLIENNE

I meant to do my work today,
But a brown bird sang in the apple tree,
And a butterfly flitted across the field,
And all the leaves were calling me.

And the wind/ went sighing over the land, 5
Tossing the grasses to and fro,
And a rainbow held out its shining hand —
So what could I do but laugh and go?

PAIR III

Dreams

LANGSTON HUGHES

Hold fast to dreams
For if dreams die
Life is a broken-winged bird
That cannot fly.

Hold fast to dreams 5
For when dreams go
Life is a barren field
Frozen with snow.

I Saw a Man Pursuing the Horizon

STEPHEN CRANE

I saw a man pursuing the horizon;
Round and round they sped.
I was disturbed at this;
I accosted the man.
"It is futile," I said,   5
"You can never——"

"You lie," he cried,
And ran on.

PAIR IV

Fog

CARL SANDBURG

The fog comes
on little cat feet.

It sits looking
over harbor and city
on silent haunches   5
and then moves on.

Sea Lullaby

ELINOR WYLIE

The old moon is tarnished
With smoke of the flood,
The dead leaves are varnished
With colour like blood,

A treacherous smiler
With teeth white as milk,
A savage beguiler
In sheathings of silk,

The sea creeps to pillage,
She leaps on her prey;
A child of the village
Was murdered today.

She came up to meet him
In a smooth golden cloak,
She choked him and beat him
To death, for a joke.

Her bright locks were tangled,
She shouted for joy,
With one hand she strangled
A strong little boy.

Now in silence she lingers
Beside him all night
To wash her long fingers
In silvery light.

PAIR V

A Vagabond's Song

BLISS CARMAN

There is something in the autumn which is native to my blood —
Touch of manner, hint of mood;
And my heart is like a rhyme,
With the yellow and the purple and the crimson keeping time.

The scarlet of the maples can shake me like a cry 5
Of bugles going by.
And my lonely spirit thrills
To see the frosty asters like a smoke upon the hills.

There is something in October sets the gyspy blood astir;
We must rise and follow her, 10
When from every hill of flame
She calls and calls each vagabond by name.

A Leaf Treader

ROBERT FROST

I have been treading on leaves all day until I am autumn-
tired.
God knows all the color and form of leaves I have trodden on
and mired.
Perhaps I have put forth too much strength and been too fierce
from fear.
I have safely trodden underfoot the leaves of another year.

All summer long they were overhead, more lifted up than I. 5
To come to their final place in earth they had to pass me by.
All summer long I thought I heard them threatening under
their breath.
And when they came it seemed with a will to carry me with
them to death.

They spoke to the fugitive in my heart as if it were leaf to leaf.
They tapped at my eyelids and touched my lips with an in-
vitation to grief. 10
But it was no reason I had to go because they had to go.
Now up my knee to keep on top of another year of snow.

Prospice

ROBERT BROWNING

Fear death? — to feel the fog in my throat,
    The mist in my face,
When the snows begin, and the blasts denote
    I am nearing the place,
The power of the night, the press of the storm,   5
    The post of the foe;
Where he stands, the Arch Fear in a visible form,
    Yet the strong man must go:
For the journey is done and the summit attained,
    And the barriers fall,   10
Though a battle's to fight ere the guerdon be gained,
    The reward of it all.
I was ever a fighter, so — one fight more,
    The best and the last!
I would hate that death bandaged my eyes and forebore,   15
    And bade me creep past.
No! let me taste the whole of it, fare like my peers
    The heroes of old,
Bear the brunt, in a minute pay glad life's arrears
    Of pain, darkness, and cold.   20
For sudden the worst turns the best to the brave,
    The black minute's at end,
And the elements' rage, the fiend-voices that rave,
    Shall dwindle, shall blend,
Shall change, shall become first a peace out of pain,   25
    Then a light, then thy breast,
O thou soul of my soul! I shall clasp thee again,°
    And with God be the rest!

26–27. In these lines Browning is referring to his wife, who died
    a short time before the poem was written.

Crossing the Bar

ALFRED, LORD TENNYSON

Sunset and evening star,
   And one clear call for me!
And may there be no moaning of the bar,°
   When I put out to sea,

But such a tide as moving seems asleep,   5
   Too full for sound and foam,
When that which drew from out the boundless deep
   Turns again home.

Twilight and evening bell,
   And after that the dark!   10
And may there be no sadness of farewell,
   When I embark;

For though from out our bourne ° of Time and Place
   The flood may bear me far,
I hope to see my Pilot face to face   15
   When I have crost the bar.

  3. **bar:** a bank of sand or gravel across the mouth of a river.
13. **bourne:** realm.

Index of Writers

Index of Writing Skills

Sentences (*cont.*)
  sentence beginnings, 143–44
  sentence lengths, 66–67
  simple sentences, 107–08

Simile, 49–50, 60

Simple sentences, variety in, 107–08

Topic sentence, 8–15
  beginning a paragraph with, 9–12
  concluding a paragraph with, 12–13
  with a clincher sentence, 14–15

Transitional expressions
  in expository compositions, 118, 123
  in paragraphs, 36–38
  in a persuasive essay, 167

Unity in paragraphs, 3–7
  descriptive, 3–4
  expository, 6–7
  narrative, 5–6

Vantage point in description, 58–63
  moving, 60–63
  stationary, 58–60

Variety
  in sentence beginnings, 143–44
  in sentence lengths, 66–67
  in simple sentences, 107–08

Verbs, use of vivid, 49, 57, 90

Words, choice of
  adjectives, 210–11
  appealing to the senses, 55–56
  creating a humorous effect, 201
  expressing an attitude, 137–38, 167–68
  figurative language, 49–50, 60, 204
  synonyms, 157
  technical terms, 163
  vivid verbs, 49, 55–56, 57

Writing about literature, *see* Literature